Successful Dissertations and Theses

DAVID MADSEN

Successful Dissertations and Theses

A GUIDE TO
GRADUATE STUDENT
RESEARCH
FROM PROPOSAL
TO COMPLETION

SECOND EDITION

Jossey-Bass Publishers • San Francisco

SUCCESSFUL DISSERTATIONS AND THESES
A Guide to Graduate Student Research from Proposal to Completion
by David Madsen

Copyright © 1992 by: Jossey-Bass Inc., Publishers
350 Sansome Street
San Francisco, California 94104

Jossey-Bass is a registered trademark of Jossey-Bass Inc., A Wiley Company.

Library of Congress Cataloging-in-Publication Data

Madsen, David.
    Successful dissertations and theses : a guide to graduate student research from proposal to completion / David Madsen. — 2nd ed.
        p. cm. — (Jossey-Bass higher and adult education series)
(Jossey-Bass social and behavioral science series)
    Includes bibliographical references (p.   ) and index.
    ISBN 1-55542-389-2
    1. Dissertations, Academic—Handbooks, manuals, etc. 2. Research—Handbooks, manuals, etc. 3. Report writing—Handbooks, manuals, etc. I. Title. II. Series. III. Series: Jossey-Bass social and behavioral science series.
    LB2369.M32 1992
    808′.02 — dc20 (alk. paper)   91-21687
                                                                CIP

Manufactured in the United States of America

SECOND EDITION

PB Printing   10 9 8

A joint publication in
The Jossey-Bass
Higher and Adult Education Series
and
The Jossey-Bass
Social and Behavioral Science Series

CONTENTS

----

ix

PREFACE

This book is the revised and expanded second edition of a volume published in 1983. The new edition of *Successful Dissertations and Theses* retains all the material of continuing relevance from the first edition—updated and reedited to enhance clarity, coherence, and economy of expression—and adds new material, particularly on the use of computers. In organization (except for the repositioning of one chapter), format, and objectives, this second edition mirrors the first edition. It also expresses my continuing belief that a comprehensive guide such as this one is needed, as well as my unequivocal enthusiasm for what a well-researched and well-written dissertation can accomplish. Consequently, portions of the preface to the first edition may bear repeating here.

Almost everyone in the academic community numbers among his acquaintances a bright, able, hard-working scholar who has completed all the requirements for an advanced degree save one: the dissertation. At some stage in its preparation, the manuscript was laid aside for one reason or another, usually with the expectation that it would soon be resumed. Yet there it remains—unfinished, unforgotten; a source of intense frustration and disappointment; a reproachful reminder of wasted time, money, and intellectual effort. Facetious references to the "A.B.D." (all-but-dissertation) often cloak the bitter acknowledgment of unfulfilled aspirations and altered career plans.

Fortunately, the syndrome that produces the A.B.D. is less likely to afflict the candidate who is well prepared, who understands what is expected of him at each stage of the degree program, and who knows how to go about researching and writing the thesis. My purpose in preparing this guide is to offer specific advice that will allay at least a portion of the natural apprehension you may be experiencing as you begin the dissertation process and to anticipate many of the problems that may arise as your task proceeds. My suggestions for a systematic but not mechanical approach to the writing of the thesis or dissertation have been designed with doctoral and master's degree candidates in mind; however, they should also prove useful to the writer of scholarly reports, essays, and papers.

. . . I consider the dissertation or thesis to be potentially one of the most significant elements of the entire higher education experience. If my recommendations can make this process more satisfying, more enriching, and generally more rewarding for students and their mentors, I shall be content.

Overview of Contents

As the table of contents indicates, I offer advice on a variety of topics: finding a subject; taking notes; outlining, writing, and defending the thesis; finding a publisher; and—most important of all—formulating the research question and preparing the research proposal.

Chapter One includes a comparison of the master's thesis and the doctoral dissertation and identifies some obstacles that can hinder students in the successful achievement of their goal. It also gives suggestions on the special guides that will be of particular use throughout the dissertation-writing process. Finally, it explains why students should, at the outset, acquire a working knowledge of the computer.

Chapter Two presents thoughts on the role of the adviser and the advisory committee: How does the student find an adviser who will give the support and help that will be needed? How are advisory committees appointed? Should the committee include a research specialist?

Chapter Three deals with the selection of the research topic and offers suggestions on how to shape it in language that will help it appear to best advantage. I suggest a specific method of casting the research question, an approach that some may find controversial. Indeed, a colleague, intending no compliment, has observed, "You are trying to take the mystery out of thesis writing." The mystery, yes — but certainly neither the excitement nor the challenge inherent in the task.

Chapter Four comes to grips with the research proposal — in my view the most important element in achieving mastery of the dissertation process. I discuss each step of the proposal and include examples of the various steps, using material from one of the sample proposals provided in the resource section (Resource A).

Chapter Five offers general suggestions for conducting research, taking notes, photocopying, preparing tables and charts, and the like.

Chapter Six, "Using the Library and Locating Essential Resources," may strike some readers as superfluous. Graduate students, they might argue, know all there is to be known on this topic. My observations lead me to disagree strongly on this point. Although some students may need little advice, a surprisingly large number have never really tapped the library's rich store of materials, never availed themselves of its services, including computer and bibliographical aids.

Chapter Seven, on "Organizing, Outlining, and Writing," deals with putting the note cards in order, making an outline, composing the first and subsequent drafts, preparing the abstract, and typing the manuscript.

Chapter Eight offers advice on defending the dissertation at the final oral examination. What can you, the candidate, expect of the examining committee? What is the background of this academic ritual? How should you conduct yourself as you face your examiners?

Chapter Nine provides suggestions on seeking a wider audience for your completed manuscript. Matters explored here include finding a publisher or, if that fails, converting the dissertation into an acceptable journal article or presenting the paper at a convention or a job interview. The chapter also raises some ethical problems involved in authorship.

The resource section contains excerpts from two thesis proposals (one, shown as Resource B, an authentic proposal; the other, Resource A, a simulated one, based on my own research), as well as a number of sample pages (Resource C), such as the first page of a completed dissertation (my own) and a sample essay bibliography.

My examples throughout are drawn primarily from disciplines in the social sciences and humanities; nevertheless, I am confident that most of my recommendations will be applicable to any academic or professional discipline. Whenever possible, I include exhibits from actual manuscripts to illustrate my recommendations.

Purpose of the Second Edition: New Materials and Approaches

When the first edition of this book appeared, I was convinced of the importance of the doctoral dissertation and the master's thesis. Today I am more enthusiastic than ever. The doctoral dissertation in particular—of which some 32,000 are completed each year—seems to be a more important piece of work than is commonly recognized. After a year-long study of fifty universities in the United States and Canada, the Council of Graduate Schools reported as follows:

> There is no question that, in the view of the faculty, students, and administrators participating in this study, the doctoral dissertation, as a demonstration of a student's ability to carry out research independently, defines the essence of the Ph.D. degree. Furthermore, with few exceptions, the dissertation in its traditional form, that is, as a document that describes in detail the research that was carried out and the results obtained, the relationship of that research to previously reported work in the field, and the significance of the research in furthering understanding of the issues in question, continues to represent the model in all fields [Council of Graduate Schools, 1991, p. 31].

Along with recognition of the importance of the dissertation, however, there is also a growing concern about the amount of time students spend in graduate school. Theodore Ziolkowski, dean of the graduate school at Princeton, summarizes the problem in these words:

> In a certain sense, our national future depends on the graduate schools. But it is also in the urgent interest of the nation at large to see that the universities recruit and retain graduate students of excellence in every field from Assyriology to astrophysics, and train them within a reasonable time to assume an appropriate place in a college or university. If universities continue to permit or require students to spend ever longer portions of the most productive period of their lives in graduate school, then the students entering graduate school this year will not yet be finished by the time of the excess demand predicted for the years 1997–2002 [Ziolkowski, 1990, p. 195].

I share Dean Ziolkowski's concern, but—thanks to the widespread availability of the personal computer—I find reason to hope that some of the routine work associated with writing a dissertation will be reduced and, even more important, the quality of dissertations enhanced. For example, when used as a word processor, the computer enables the writer to make corrections with ease, and laser printers produce superb copies in any quantity desired. In addition, there are "spelling checkers," thesauruses, and even "grammar checkers" (for those who want them) to ease the writer's path.

More important, however, is the fact that computers—with their ability to tap hundreds of databases—make literature searches easier to conduct. Many American universities employ CD-ROM (Compact Disk–Read Only Memory) devices to search for relevant periodicals, dissertations, books, encyclopedias, and other resources; and even these advances are being superseded, so that scholars can tap directly into computer-stored information on campus or the other side of the country without ever leaving their desks. Computers also make it possible for scholars to analyze and organize data quickly and accurately, carry out alternative analyses, and conduct simulation exercises. Finally, many scholars these days are communicating with one another — exchanging ideas and information — through the electronic mail capabilities of the computer.

In revising this book, then, I have taken into account the advances made in computers, especially the personal and laptop varieties. I have added to Chapter One a section on learning to use a computer; I have included a discussion of the mechanics of a computer search for dissertation topics in Chapter Three; and I have added a section on computer services to Chapter Six. Nevertheless, certain cautions are in order. Because the computer is a fascinating tool, a student can be beguiled into forgetting the dissertation in order to explore the software available. Another caution stems from the fact that the computer industry, whether it deals with hardware or software, is probably the fastest moving in the world today, so that advice given this morning may be obsolete this afternoon. Finally, it must never be forgotten that, despite the wonders of which the computer is capable, preparing a dissertation requires thought, planning, and careful attention to detail. When he had surveyed all the marvels on display at a campus "computer fair," a colleague of mine wryly acknowledged that his favorite computer was still his "Ticonderoga 2" — a number 2 lead pencil.

No matter what is said about the wonders (and flaws) of the computer and its radiant potential for the future, the heart of this revised book remains where it was in the first edition: in the selection and shaping of the research topic and the preparation of the research proposal (Chapters Three and Four). To this end, I have suggested new approaches to finding a research topic. I have also, I believe, devised a better way to explain relationships and their applicability to research. I have sought and found additional examples of research questions, especially those of a more complex type. Moreover, I have read a hundred or so dissertations in the past eight years with an eye to their strengths and weaknesses; I hope what I have learned has permeated these pages.

Aided by advice from students and publishers, I have expanded the chapter on publishing the dissertation and have added what I believe to be helpful suggestions on the presentation of the dissertation at the job interview. I have expanded and updated the chapter on using the library, added new references, and made other changes throughout the manuscript. Above all, I have tried not to give too much advice; too much advice, I believe, is worse than too little.

Two criticisms of the first edition deserve special comment. A scholar from abroad said that because the book was written with American students in mind some of my counsel might not meet the needs of foreign students. I acknowledge the truth of this criticism, for although I have worked with foreign students and have spent time in a foreign university, I did have American graduate students in mind as I wrote. I am convinced, however, that a sound research question and a systematic procedure know no nationality and are much the same the world over.

A second criticism was that while the book provided guidance to students in the humanities, social sciences, and professional schools, it placed less emphasis on engineering and the physical and biological sciences. Part of the reason is that those disciplines elicit a greater variety of dissertations. In a publication entitled *The Role and Nature of the Doctoral Dissertation: A Policy Statement*, the Council of Graduate Schools addresses this issue as follows: "In engineering and the physical and biological sciences, which are increasingly team disciplines with large groups of investigators working on common problems, dissertations often present, in varied formats, the results of several independent but related experiments" (1991, p. 13). The council adds: "How a discipline normally conducts its work is distinctly reflected in that discipline's expectations for the Ph.D. dissertation" (1991, p. 14). The new edition of this book does include more examples drawn from the biological and physical sciences. Students interested in additional reading in engineering and in the biological and physical sciences might explore the reference section for the works of Barrass (1978, 1982), Davis (1980), Dixon (1973), Katz (1985), Kronick (1985), Lansbury (1975), Michaelson (1986), Remington and Schork (1985), and especially the second edition of Robert V. Smith's *Graduate Research: A Guide for Students in the Sciences* (1990).

Terminology

I use the words *thesis* and *dissertation* synonymously throughout the chapters. I do so for two reasons. First, although some universities employ the term *dissertation* for the Ph.D. manuscript only and reserve *thesis* for the master's paper, many others use the terms interchangeably. Harvard, in fact, seems to prefer *thesis*; Chicago, *dissertation*. There is no hard-and-fast rule regarding the distinction. Second and more important, I believe that the master's paper (however it is titled, and though narrower in scope and content than the doctoral manuscript) demands the same systematic approach to research and writing as the Ph.D. document.

Acknowledgments

In the preparation of the second edition, I am especially grateful for the help given me by Charles Burgess, Elizabeth L. Feetham, Lester Goodchild, Augustine McCaffery, Jane Sanders, Robert E. Tostberg, Peter Van de Water, Donald T. Williams, and Robert Williams. Loretta Lopez of the University of Washington Library and Gale W. Erlandson, Dorothy Conway, and Susan Abel of Jossey-Bass have given me invaluable advice. From start to finish, Lois Fox Madsen has been my collaborator.

Seattle, Washington David Madsen
September 1991

THE AUTHOR

David Madsen is professor of education at the University of Washington. He has also taught at the University of Michigan and Teachers College, Columbia University. He received his Ph.B. degree (1951) from the University of North Dakota, his A.M. degree (1954) from the University of Chicago, and his Ph.D. degree (1961) from the University of Chicago in education. In 1967–68 he was a national postdoctoral fellow in education research at the University of California, Berkeley. In 1983 he was a visiting professor at the University of Bergen in Norway.

In addition to journal articles, monographs, reviews, and the first edition of *Successful Dissertations and Theses*, published in 1983, Madsen has written *The National University: Enduring Dream of the U.S.A.* (1966), *Early National Education, 1776–1830* (1974), and an article, "The History and Philosophy of Higher Education," for the *Encyclopedia of Educational Research* (5th ed., 1982). Besides being interested in policies affecting graduate education, Madsen is a student of the history of American colleges and universities in the twentieth century.

Successful
Dissertations
and Theses

1

Starting
and Completing
the Dissertation

What is a doctoral dissertation? The question sounds simple enough, and yet it really isn't easy to find the precise words to describe the dissertation. The Council of Graduate Schools, for example, gives the following definition:

> [The Ph.D. dissertation] fulfills two major purposes: (1) it is an intensive, highly professional training experience, the successful completion of which demonstrates the candidate's ability to address a major intellectual problem and arrive at a successful conclusion independently and at a high level of professional competence, and (2) its results constitute an original contribution to knowledge in the field [Council of Graduate Schools, 1990a, p. 21].

The statement raises several questions. What kinds of *results* will constitute a truly "original contribution to knowledge"? What does the word *independently* mean in this context? Surely most people who write dissertations get help of one kind or other; indeed, "help of one kind or other" is what books such as this one are supposed to give. And just how *high* is a "high level of professional competence"? Inevitably, perhaps, research advisers and supervisory committee members are responsible for providing answers to these questions. Inevitably, too, there will be a difference of opinion on both the precise meaning of each term and the priority each deserves. Obviously, students will be keenly interested in how their advisers and supervisory committee members answer these questions.

The foregoing statement also raises a subtle question about the fundamental purpose of the dissertation. Nor is the question a new one. In 1960 Bernard Berelson asked: "Should the doctoral dissertation be regarded more as a training instrument than as an 'original contribution to knowledge'?" (p. 174). The council's definition suggests that the dissertation should accomplish both these purposes: it should provide an "intensive, highly professional training experience"; and at the same time its results should "constitute an original contribution to knowledge." Although both purposes are clearly difficult to assess, the second—with its demands for an "original contribution"—is more difficult to grasp and for that reason, perhaps, is more controversial. "In its most general sense," the Council of Graduate Schools asserted in 1991, "'original' describes research that has not been done previously or a project that creates new knowledge; it implies that there is some novel twist, fresh perspective, new hypothesis, or innovative method that makes the dissertation project a distinctive contribution" (pp. 8–9).

Many scholars look upon graduate study as "intensive, highly professional training." In their view the dissertation serves primarily as a demonstration of a candidate's ability to handle the tools and ideas necessary to conduct research; therefore, it is a waste of time to argue the irrefutable meaning of "original contribution." Other scholars agree that graduate study should be "intensive, highly professional training"; they insist, however, that the dissertation, independently conceived and executed, should be an original and significant contribution to knowledge. Anything less, they argue, results in lower standards.

In an effort to address the difficult issue of scope, the Council of Graduate Schools (1990a, p. 22) wrote as follows:

> The allowable scope of the dissertation project is difficult to state precisely. The dissertation should clearly be a substantial and significant undertaking, yet not so extensive or open-ended that it cannot be successfully concluded in a reasonable period of time. The trend in recent years has been away

from the long and comprehensive dissertation project, and in the direction of a more sharply delineated task requiring perhaps a year to two years of full-time productive effort. The dissertation should be the introduction to a career of research and scholarship, not its apex.

It is doubtless true that only a few dissertations qualify as masterpieces. A good many, however, establish the foundation for a lifetime of scholarship. When Porter and his colleagues studied a random sample of 645 doctorates awarded in six disciplines (physics, biochemistry, zoology, electrical engineering, psychology, and sociology), they concluded that "the dissertation is far more than a mundane academic hurdle. It results in publication in half of the cases, yielding on average one directly derived publication per dissertation, and these publications are cited more often than others by the same authors" (1982, p. 478).

Doctoral and Master's Theses: A Comparison

What is the purpose and scope of the master's thesis? How does it differ from the doctoral dissertation? Why have some departments discontinued the master's thesis as a requirement? Why have some departments abandoned the master's degree? Why do some look upon it as a terminal degree awarded to those who do not proceed to the doctorate?

Easy answers to these questions are not to be had, in part because the master's degree itself has been controversial throughout the twentieth century. As Judith S. Glazer puts it: "The master's degree is the mainspring of graduate education, the first postbaccalaureate degree, the midpoint to the doctorate—and the terminal degree for most professions. Beyond this generalization, little agreement exists about its goals and objectives, functions and purposes, curricula and criteria for evaluation" (1986, p. 1).

As early as 1909, Glazer (p. 9) reports, the Association of American Universities (AAU) commissioned a study of the master's degree and "found little standardization of requirements for either admission or the degree." In 1935 the AAU tried again; this time a committee "described the master's as a research degree, a professional degree, a teacher's degree, and a culture degree" and recommended one year of graduate study in a unified program of graduate courses, culminating in a final examination and original thesis. (At the time, only one half of AAU members required either an examination or a thesis.)"

Today little has changed. Approximately one-third of the colleges and universities in the United States offer graduate programs of one sort or other. In 1987–88 about 300,000 master's degrees were awarded, roughly two-thirds of them in education, business and management, engineering and engineering technologies, allied health and health sciences, and public affairs and social work. How many specialties and subspecialties all these degrees represented, and how many of the successful candidates for the degree submitted a thesis, can only be conjectured. Some candidates were in programs that required no thesis; others were in programs that required a "paper," a "report," a "special project," or a "research report." One would need to examine the bulletins of hundreds of colleges and universities to determine precisely what was required for the degree.

What advice, then, can one give to someone about to undertake the preparation of a master's thesis? Perhaps the main difference between the master's thesis and the doctoral dissertation is scope, but again we encounter a certain degree of imprecision. In an effort to describe the "scope" of the doctoral dissertation, the Council of Graduate Schools advised "a year to two years of full-time productive effort" (1990a, p. 22). If a year or two is recommended for the doctoral dissertation, surely something less is appropriate for the master's thesis; how much less is difficult to say. Once again the adviser and supervisory committee (if there is one) must be relied on for advice. In general, however, the author of a master's thesis should demonstrate independent ability to address and solve a serious intellectual problem, albeit one that is less ambitious than that addressed by the doctoral dissertation.

One way to control the scope of the master's thesis is to reduce the number of concepts, events, phenomena, variables, or things under study. For example, instead of studying the interaction among children and teachers in an elementary school for a semester, one might study the interaction of fourth-grade children in one classroom for one week. Or, instead of studying the alteration of major European traditions in America, one might study changes of two German folkways among the German-American citizens of St. Louis in the nineteenth century. Or, instead of analyzing geological and biological variables and their interaction, one might study the effect a change in temperature has on a bacterium found in desert soil in Arizona. Whether or not these examples would be acceptable as topics for master's theses, they are limited. All the same, authorities in each field might insist that such topics, although they appear to be limited in scope, are in fact quite complex and if approached correctly might even qualify as doctoral theses.

Should the master's thesis also represent an original and substantial contribution to knowledge? Yes, within reason and without demanding an excessive amount of time and effort on the part of the candidate.

Because there are many similarities in the purposes and procedures of master's theses and doctoral dissertations, much of the advice given for writing the doctoral dissertation pertains to writing the master's thesis as well. Indeed, many doctoral dissertations are matured master's theses, or the product of ideas developed in the process of writing a thesis. For example, Thomas M. Doerflinger's *A Vigorous Spirit of Enterprise: Merchants and Economic Development in Revolutionary Philadelphia,* awarded the Bancroft Prize in American History in 1986, began as research for an undergraduate thesis at Princeton. Doerflinger reported, moreover, that his father's doctoral dissertation at Harvard, on the subject of sea chanteys, began as a senior thesis at Princeton (*Chronicle of Higher Education,* April 1, 1987, p. 3.).

It seems clear that anyone who undertakes a doctoral dissertation after having written a serious bachelor's or master's thesis has a clear advantage over someone who lacks that experience; even so, caution is recommended lest the topic chosen be too ambitious, and, as already noted, the adviser is in the best position to assess the prudence of what is proposed.

A.B.D.s, or "The Schubert Society"

In Great Britain, I am told, students who have completed all the requirements for the doctorate except the dissertation are some-

times said to be members of "The Schubert Society," a wry
characterization inspired by that composer's Symphony No. 8 in
B Minor, the "Unfinished." Students fail to complete the dissertation for a number of reasons: money runs short; ennui sets in;
illness, marital discord, and other personal problems make
concentration difficult; the dissertation topic proves elusive or
unmanageable; enthusiasm wanes. Granted, some students
make an honest and realistic appraisal of their interests and
talents and conclude that the game is not worth the candle. In
most cases, however, the explanation is not so straightforward,
and other reasons must be sought, often in the student's personal makeup. In the next few pages, we shall consider some of
the characteristics or circumstances that can impede progress
toward completion of the degree. The cases in point are the ones
most commonly encountered; undoubtedly, the list could be
expanded. Ponder the following descriptions carefully: does any
strike a familiar chord?

Too Soon Adieu. Were I obliged to limit myself to a single bit of
advice to a graduate student, it would be this: If you can possibly
manage to do so, remain at the university until the dissertation is
finished.

Many forces will conspire to send you out of the academic
environment before your task is done. Economic necessity: it's
hard to ignore a depleted bank account. An irresistible job
opportunity: your every instinct tells you to seize it. Boredom or
a sense of stagnation: the first fine careless rapture is gone;
maybe a stint in the outside world will help restore your jaded
intellectual appetites. Besides, you tell yourself, a full-time job
will absorb only part of your waking hours, leaving plenty of
time and opportunity to finish the dissertation. Unfortunately,
things seldom work out as we expect them to. The distractions of
a new job and new surroundings can siphon off energy that
should be concentrated on the dissertation. And the entire
project may seem less urgent, even less significant, than it did
while you were on campus. Somewhat less difficulty is reported
by students who have found employment in academe. Even as
full-time teaching or research assistants, most are able to devote

some time each day to completing the thesis, perhaps because the ambience is more conducive to intellectual effort than is the office or marketplace.

If you cannot remain in residence while finishing the manuscript, make every effort to get as much done as possible before you depart. Once away from the campus, you will have to summon up all your reserves of self-discipline to keep at the task. At least five days a week without fail, try to do some writing on the dissertation. (Many students find early morning the best time to work uninterrupted.) Even if you can spare only thirty minutes a day, you will see slow but sure progress toward your goal. At all costs, resist the temptation to shelve the thesis temporarily when other more enticing prospects intervene. Never attempt to assuage your guilt with the promise "I'll get back on track right after the holidays (or next summer, or next year . . .)."

Too Much Enthusiasm, Too Little Focus. Interested and enthusiastic students gladden the heart of every teacher. They leap into graduate study with the same boundless energy they bring to all other aspects of their lives. In their search for a dissertation topic, they are likely to turn up a hundred ideas, several of which will prove worthy of pursuit. Consider one such young woman who visits the library to collect material for a paper on Erasmus. In no time she is enmeshed in Renaissance art, religion, and politics and in the biographies of Martin Luther and Thomas More. Many of the ideas she encounters have only a tangential association with Erasmus; nevertheless, her great energy may lead her to pursue them all, sometimes to the point of ignoring her original topic. One of her great virtues — enthusiasm — becomes a potential vice when it stands in the way of selecting a dissertation topic, imposing appropriate limits on it, and finishing the work in a reasonable length of time.

Some advisers — myself among them — are captivated by the enthusiastic student. The avid pursuit of knowledge deserves to be encouraged, we feel, not constrained. At the same time, we must recognize our responsibility to see the student's energy and enthusiasm directed toward a specific target — the dissertation — rather than allowing it to be unprofitably diffused.

Too Hard to Please. A few students never finish the dissertation precisely because they cannot persuade themselves that it is possible to bring the manuscript to the desired state of perfection. One more chapter . . . a little more tinkering with the conclusions . . . more citations . . . more examples . . . and so on, ad infinitum. Some perfectionists have been known to snatch the rough draft from the typists to make "a few little changes" and have finally relinquished it months or even years later. In extreme cases neither the typist nor the members of the advisory committee ever see it again.

These same students often have great difficulty in choosing a topic: somehow, nothing is ever quite right. Once again, advisers can be of great help if they recognize the difficulty. Often they must exercise great patience, for some students will need more time than others to complete the dissertation, and it is not always a simple matter to determine how much time should be allowed. Some students are comfortable working under a deadline, especially if it is one over which they have little control, as when an adviser announces: "I am going on sabbatical leave next year; I suggest you finish the final draft by February at the latest so we can schedule the examination in March or April."

Too Casual. Oddly enough, the perfectionist's opposite also can have difficulty with the dissertation. Consider the excellent student who dashes off good term papers—wham-bam!—in the wee hours of the morning, gets *A*'s, and finds schooling a breeze. This type of scholar can usually write a first draft that would be acceptable as a term paper. But when it comes to the writing of the dissertation, it is a different matter entirely. Here is an academic experience for which the habit of dashing off term papers late at night is the poorest possible preparation. The first draft is seldom good enough; moreover, hasty work or careless thought in the proposal or dissertation is quickly apparent to the advisory committee, which may respond in a negative manner, either posing challenging questions or offering unexpected resistance to what the candidate is trying to do. With his quick wits and facility in writing, the "wham-bammer" is capable of fine and original work if he can persuade himself to break old habits and approach the dissertation with the respect and dedication it deserves.

Too Compulsive. Some students are exhaustive note takers, filling file boxes, shoe boxes, cartons, and closets with note cards. Thoroughness is all very well; but when it becomes compulsiveness, it may cloak a desire to avoid the act of synthesis the dissertation requires. To be sure, term papers and examinations require synthesis, too, but seldom to the degree the dissertation does. Moreover, the dissertation is a public act; a proposal must be prepared for examination by a committee; the final manuscript must undergo scrutiny and eventually find a place on a library shelf for all the world to read. Usually, too, the author of a dissertation must present his topic to friends and fellow students in seminar. The public aspects of the dissertation process can be surprisingly painful to persons who dislike tying the ends together or who put a high price on their privacy.

Too Long in Transit. Thesis writing seems to bring out the procrastinator in all of us. There is probably no mystery about it: we all fear failure, but many of us also fear success, for we know that more will be expected of us if we succeed. The safest thing, then, is to hover somewhere between success and failure, always remaining in transit. Many universities have a stipulation that the dissertation must be completed within ten years. The candidate either finishes in a reasonable length of time or risks being perceived as a failure.

Occasionally, draconian measures may be required. One writer describes a successful scheme adopted by a young assistant professor of mathematics to force herself to complete her doctoral thesis. Following a friend's suggestion, she placed five dollars in each of ten envelopes addressed to an institution she particularly disliked. If she failed to write five or more pages of the thesis during a given week, an envelope was to be mailed to the institution. By the eighth week, she had a draft ready for her committee and had forfeited only two payments. When she delayed making minor revisions suggested by her committee, she tried the same technique for a three-week period, with an added spur in the form of a note inviting a representative of the despised object of her beneficence to call on her. Within six days she had made the revisions, and a short time later her degree was awarded (Harris, 1974).

In one university a small group of students working on dissertations meets regularly in an effort to provide mutual aid over periods of inactivity. Some of the tactics employed are similar to those of Alcoholics Anonymous, with each student facing up to the problem of procrastination. During these eight-week group sessions, counselors, as well as the participants themselves, offer advice on more efficient use of time, and everyone attempts to approach the task of dissertation writing in a positive, rather than a self-condemnatory, frame of mind.

Too Much Independence. One reason some students never finish the dissertation stems from the structured nature of the academic environment itself. These students do not finish precisely because the process demands a high degree of independence and self-motivation. Unfortunately, formal schooling, which advances according to schedules and deadlines, does not necessarily foster qualities such as independence or creativity. For the student's first twelve years of schooling, most of it compulsory, everything is arranged. Classes meet according to the clock, terms begin and end according to schedule, course work must be completed within fixed deadlines, and examinations are taken at stated intervals.

It is not until the scholar reaches graduate school that the burden of this schedule is partially relaxed. How disconcerting, then, at the end of years of formal schooling to come abruptly to the doctoral dissertation. Except for the usual time limit for its completion, there are few instructions, few deadlines, few strictures, and sometimes only a modicum of active encouragement from others. Many students thrive under this new freedom; they take on the assignment with relish, complete it with dispatch, and cast about for new independent research tasks to accomplish. Yet for those who have been conditioned to rely too heavily on schedules imposed on them by others, the dissertation work may drag along until they have exhausted their sources of financial support. When that occurs, graduate study often must be abandoned altogether.

Unfortunately, there is little agreement in the matter of how much independence graduate students should be granted. Some authorities would allow wider latitude in choice of dissertation topic (Heiss, 1970, pp. 286–287; Mayhew, 1972, p. 181; Harvey, 1972, p. 64). On the other hand, exhortations on behalf of greater guidance, sometimes from the same sources, are plentiful: "Maximum guidance for the student in the choice of his topic and the design of his research should be afforded by dissertation advisers. At the same time, the student's right to choose his own topic and to conduct his own research in his own fashion should not be threatened" (Harvey, 1972, p. 64). Surely there is a paradox in the concept of maximum freedom with maximum guidance.

In an unusually interesting study, Friedenberg and Roth (1954, p. 71) report that successful graduate students have "coherent, personal, intellectual purposes which they conceive as goals and actively seek. They use the university . . . as an institution which will help them get where they wish to go — where they wished to go before they had ever heard of the university and would wish to go whether or not the university existed." These students, they assert, "employ [the university] at their convenience, for purposes of their own, which are consistent with, and related to, its function." Not every student is as well motivated as the subjects of the Friedenberg and Roth study; nonetheless, everyone can benefit by approaching the dissertation with some of the same intensity and single-mindedness they demonstrated.

Too Much Isolation. "Fight isolation," writes Henry Rosovsky. "It is the greatest enemy of graduate students. Research is a lonely activity, especially when the location is a library rather than a laboratory. Few experiences in our working life can be more isolating than gathering materials for a dissertation deep in the bowels of some large library" (1990, p. 153). Although some students find solitary work highly exhilarating, Rosovsky is nevertheless correct: isolation can be a problem. One useful tactic to minimize it is to form a departmental dissertation discussion group. At regularly scheduled meetings participants describe the progress they are making on the search for a topic, the research proposal, the defense, or any part of the dissertation process. Groups of this kind can be especially valuable when the dissertation proposal is being drafted and when the dissertation is nearing completion. Graduate students can often give one another ideas and support that supplement the advice of advisers and supervisory committee members. Some university departments take the responsibility for organizing these dissertation discussion groups; some are assembled by professors. But those that grow as a result of student initiative are among the most successful.

Too Little Appreciation of the Scholarly Tradition. To participate wholeheartedly in the degree process, students must understand what they are doing and why they are doing it. Unfortunately, many go through years of graduate study without learning anything about the academic tradition of which they are a part. Most students realize that a well-written dissertation that advances human knowledge can provide one of life's most rewarding intellectual experiences, earn them the esteem of fellow scholars, and bring pride and satisfaction to family and friends. Still, at times many doctoral students find themselves wondering why they are writing a dissertation, anyway. Is it just another hurdle, or is it academically justified? It is, of course, academically justified. When students write and defend a dissertation in a university today, they become a link in the chain of scholarship reaching back to medieval times. Although the origin of the dissertation as a requirement for conferral of a degree is unknown, various possibilities have been suggested. It is known, for example, that a dissertation or defense of a thesis was a requirement for admission to the Franciscan order in the thirteenth century; the medieval university, with its close ties to the church, may simply have adopted the ecclesiastical usage (Engel, 1966, p. 781).

Moreover, parallels can be drawn with the practices of the powerful merchants' and artisans' guilds of the Middle Ages.

Today's university convocation is embellished by vestiges of both guild and clerical ceremony: the marshal's baton, the elaborate hoods and vestments, the award of degrees. Like the guild apprentices, university students were admitted to a course of study, shaped into journeymen, and finally welcomed into the company of scholars to practice their craft as teaching masters. The right to grant the license to teach — the *jus ubique docendi* — was jealously guarded by a few universities, such as Paris and Bologna, which drew their authority from the Church of Rome.

One of their requirements for licensure was a final examination or defense of a thesis against all comers, skill in disputation being regarded as one of the marks of the educated man. In effect, the early dissertation demonstrated the candidate's competence to teach, and in this sense was analogous to the "masterpiece" submitted to a jury of guild masters. Instead of producing a tangible object crafted in metal, cloth, wood, or stone, the scholar displayed verbal and intellectual skills in defending a proposition. Occasionally, the defense had two components: a private examination, in which the candidate defended his thesis against the challenges of the masters; and a public demonstration of his intellectual powers, often in the form of a lecture presented to professors, fellow students, and friends.

The terms *master, professor,* and *doctor* appear to have been more or less synonymous in the Middle Ages. In time the term *master* came to be associated with the faculty in arts (the degree itself became primarily an honorary one, as it was in eighteenth-century American colleges), and the term *doctor* with the professional schools of medicine, law, and theology (Rashdall, [1895] 1936, p. 21). In German universities of the nineteenth century, the title *doctor* became popular as a designation for all who had attained an advanced level of scholarship.

For over five centuries the disputation served as the standard test for the doctoral degree, but it gradually fell into disrepute. In the early nineteenth century, especially after the founding of the University of Berlin in 1809, the dissertation was no longer regarded as a demonstration of ability to teach; instead, it became a comprehensive exercise in original research and scholarship. It was to Berlin in particular that great numbers of American students gravitated when they went abroad in search of advanced study. In 1876, with the founding of Johns Hopkins University, research and scientific inquiry as practiced at Berlin and other German institutions were transplanted to a new academic setting, where they took root and flourished. Johns Hopkins University and other new ventures, such as the University of Chicago, founded in 1890, set the pace for graduate study and challenged the older American institutions to commit substantial resources to the improvement of graduate education. So serious was their dedication to this ideal that many educational innovators of the day entertained proposals to establish exclusively graduate enterprises. Ideas of this sort proved indefensible, however, as it was recognized that graduate students came in largest numbers from the ranks of undergraduates within the same institution. For the most part, this situation prevails today.

As a result of these prodigious efforts on behalf of graduate education, American students today — especially those enrolled at the fifty-eight institutions that comprise the Association of American Universities — have unprecedented opportunities for advanced study and research. With each new decade the number of degrees awarded in the United States has risen dramatically. In 1900, for example, about 250 doctoral degrees were awarded; in 1980 the total was 30,982. In the 130-year period from 1861 (when Yale conferred the first three Ph.D.s granted by an American university) until 1990, approximately one million candidates have earned the doctorate.

What Is at Stake?

Four distinct parties — you, the candidate; your research adviser; the university; and society as a whole — have a vital interest in the successful outcome of your thesis or dissertation project. Every time a graduate student's dissertation sheds some light on a dark corner of human understanding and banishes some segment, however small, of the world's mystery, society reaps incalculable benefits. To be sure, in the United States society also foots most of the bill for higher education. Yet if we could calculate the value of the university's contribution to human knowledge in the past century, we would no doubt judge the money well spent. And despite the fact that what qualifies as a "contribution to human understanding" is open to serious debate, there is no question that society has an essential stake in the maintenance of the highest possible standards for the doctoral dissertation.

The university itself has a vital interest in maintaining the highest quality in dissertation writing and research. When an institution grants the Doctor of Philosophy degree, it attests to the research competence of the recipient. Since the certification of competence rests, in part, on the quality of the dissertation, the university's reputation is on the line every time a candidate's work is judged acceptable by a committee of his or her professors. Similarly, the research adviser's reputation is closely bound up with the quality of the dissertations that he or she supervises.

But it is you, the student, who have the most to gain from a tautly reasoned and well-written dissertation. The material rewards, often substantial, and the prestige usually accorded the possessor of the Ph.D. may be there in abundance, but for you they will be overshadowed by the lasting satisfaction of knowing you have stretched the limits of knowledge in some field or other. You may take even more satisfaction from the sense of accomplishment that results when you have addressed a difficult problem and achieved a solution. The dissertation process should be exacting. But to the dedicated scholar it should be a rewarding and pleasurable experience as well.

A final word of caution: At its best the dissertation can be the single most interesting and instructive element in your entire formal education. Unfortunately, not everyone finds it so. Some will grow weary before completing the manuscript; others will encounter personal problems that inhibit their progress. Ill health, monetary woes, marital turbulence, for example—all have claimed their casualties when occasioned by or coupled with the intense intellectual and emotional demands of advanced scholarship. Early in your academic career, you should ask yourself whether you find the university's primary activities—research and intellectual inquiry—to your liking. If the answer is "no," you will find both the aims and methods of the university uncongenial, and the dissertation at the end of the journey will be drudgery unleavened by a sense of joy in schol-arly achievement. Although most persons with imagination, flexibility, and persistence can accommodate themselves to cir-cumstances for which they feel a certain lack of enthusiasm, the student who is completely out of sympathy with the goals and values of the university probably does not belong there. Writing a dissertation can be a rigorous experience — make no mistake. But for those of you who stay the course, it can also be one of the most exhilarating experiences of adult life, one that forces you to exercise to the fullest your capacity for hard, independent thought.

Getting Started: Special Guides

Among those who are determined to stay the course and avoid the A.B.D. stigma, a few will need some refreshment on library holdings and procedures. If you are a little rusty, you might wish to read Chapter Six, "Using the Library and Locating Essential Resources," before you continue. Even if you are thoroughly comfortable in the library and have collected all the books, monographs, periodicals, laboratory findings, manuscripts, and other materials pertaining to your research topic, you will still find that you need certain special guides and other re-sources. Some of these works you will want on your bookshelf for instant reference; others will be available in the library as needed.

In-House Guides. To be sure, no single guide can be all-sufficient as you undertake such varied tasks as posing a significant re-search question, choosing an appropriate research technique, analyzing relevant data with professional skill, and setting forth your conclusions in lucid, economical, and graceful prose. At all stages of the dissertation process, however, you will be expected to meet specific institutional requirements. At the outset, then, you must have in hand the list of guidelines published by your department, college, or graduate school. Of the 200 or more

American institutions granting the doctorate, about 70 percent make available to graduate students some sort of printed or mimeographed instructions. Whether compiled by the office of graduate studies or by individual departments or schools, these guidelines deal with such basic matters as the mechanics of typing the dissertation, time schedules for the submission of material, examination requirements, and the like.

Style and Form Manuals. In addition to such in-house guides, you will wish to consult a comprehensive manual of style and form, such as *A Manual for Writers of Term Papers, Theses, and Dissertations* (Turabian, 1987) or *Form and Style: Theses, Reports, Term Papers* (Campbell and Ballou, 1990). Social scientists often use the *Publication Manual of the American Psychological Association* (American Psychological Association, 1983). Another guide is the *MLA Handbook for Writers of Research Papers, Theses, and Dissertations* (Modern Language Association of America, 1988). Although these four guides—Turabian, Campbell and Ballou, the APA, and the MLA—are probably the most widely used, some departments prefer students to use a guide specifically prepared for the discipline. Among these are the following:

> Biology: *CBE Style Manual: A Guide for Authors, Editors, and Publishers in the Biological Sciences* (American Institute of Biological Sciences, 1978).
> Chemistry: *The ACS Style Guide: A Manual for Authors and Editors* (American Chemical Society, 1986).
> Law: *A Uniform System of Citation* (Harvard Law Review Association, 1986).
> Medicine: *Style Book and Editorial Manual* (American Medical Association, 1966).
> Physics: *Style Manual for Guidance in the Preparation of Papers for Journals Published by the American Institute of Physics* (American Institute of Physics, 1978).

A caveat: Do not wait until you are ready to write your first draft before you acquire the style manual recommended by your department or university. Get a copy as soon as you can and become familiar with it. Let me give just one reason why. Suppose your department requires use of the *Publication Manual of the American Psychological Association*. And suppose that in the course of your research you have used several dissertations from other universities, some of which you obtained through interlibrary loan and others from University Microfilms. The *Publication Manual of the American Psychological Association* requires that in both cases you give the volume and page numbers from the *Dissertation Abstracts International* as well as the University Microfilm numbers for the dissertations you ordered from Ann Arbor, Michigan. Furthermore, it requires both the year the degree was awarded and the year the dissertation abstract appears in the *Dissertation Abstracts International*. At all costs you will want to avoid the hassle of retracing your steps to hunt for numbers. The solution, of course, is to have a copy of that style manual at your elbow, so that, when the dissertations are in front of you, you can enter the necessary information on your bibliography cards or in your personal database. If your department or university requires a style manual with which you are already thoroughly familiar, you are lucky. But even then some caution is warranted, because you probably will examine sources other than books and periodicals — sources you never encountered when dashing off those undergraduate term papers late at night.

Guides to Expository Writing. Since the preceding volumes deal mainly with the mechanics of presentation, scholars who approach the dissertation as discourse will also wish to have one of the many authoritative guides to expository style. Some highly recommended works that will help hone your writing skills are *Style: Toward Clarity and Grace* (Williams, 1990), *The Elements of Style* (Strunk and White, 1979), *The Complete Plain Words* (Gowers, 1962), *Line by Line* (Cook, 1985), and *On Writing, Editing, and Publishing* (Barzun, 1986). Another suggestion, although it may seem obvious, is to dig out the latest edition of those old undergraduate books on writing that you used when you took English composition during your first year in college. Such titles might include *The Practical Stylist* (Baker, 1981), *The Holt Guide to English* (Irmscher, 1985), *Prentice-Hall Handbook for Writers* (Leggett,

Mead, and Charvat, 1988), and *Writing with a Purpose* (McCrimmon, 1988). (See also Barrass, 1982; Barzun, 1985; Katz, 1985; Lester, 1987; Luey, 1987; Van Til, 1983; Zinsser, 1988.)

Guides to Preparing Theses and Dissertations. There are a few guides—such as this one, though generally less comprehensive—designed to lead the doctoral or master's candidate through the intricacies of the dissertation process itself, from the formulation of the research question through the preparation of the manuscript and on through the oral defense of the thesis. Although it is now out of print, one of the most useful older guides of this kind is Allen's (1973) *Graduate Students' Guide to Theses and Dissertations*. Allen concisely asks and answers many questions that perplex authors of dissertations. (See also Balian, 1988; Ballou, 1970; Becker, 1986; Davis and Parker, 1979; Davis, 1980; Gardner and Beatty, 1980; Krathwohl, 1977; Long, Convey, and Chwalek, 1986; Michaelson, 1986; Mauch and Birch, 1989; Smith, 1990; Sternberg, 1981.)

A Recommendation: Learn to Use a Computer

Long before you are ready to discuss a proposal for a dissertation topic with your research adviser, you should acquire a computer and master its three prime functions: as a word processor; as a device with which to seek, transfer, store, analyze, and display data; and as a medium of communication. I make this strong recommendation because I am convinced that when students fully employ the remarkable powers of the computer, better dissertations will be the result.

The computer has given scholars freedom to devote time and energy to the investigation of topics and concerns once considered unmanageable because of the quantities of information that had to be digested and analyzed. Like the photocopier, the computer is a tool or mechanical slave; but unlike the photocopier, which is relatively simple to operate, the computer demands certain skills on the part of the user. While years of study and application are required to attain the highest levels of skill in statistics, mathematics, and computer science, a modest investment of time and energy will yield satisfactory results for the dissertation writer. Fortunately, the skills that will take you a long way in the use of computers can be acquired in a surprisingly short time.

Many students are already comfortable with the computer. Some, however, may have been intimidated by the intense fervor of computer zealots, especially recent converts, or were disappointed in their initial efforts to take up this powerful tool. If so, they should give it another try. Computers are much more "user friendly" than just a few years ago, and they are within the price range of almost everyone.

Most universities regularly offer short courses on the operation of the computer for both students and faculty, and computer centers maintain small libraries on their use and employ people who can give expert advice. My university, for example, publishes a list of courses and workshops on computers and computing; many are free and have no prerequisites except the ability to type. For some, no registration is required. Some are for beginners, others for intermediate or advanced students. The subjects include introduction to IBM PCs and compatibles, Apple Macintoshes, and others; many deal with specific software programs, statistics, spreadsheets, databases, networking, and on and on. There is a course called "Introduction to LATEX," for example, that will teach you how to format dissertations and scientific papers, particularly if they include mathematical formulas. There are video training programs that allow you to use videotapes to teach yourself on a self-paced basis. There are user groups that meet regularly and are free and open to the public; no matter what kind of computer you have, chances are there is a user group to which you might belong.

If you wish to teach yourself the rudiments of this subject, there are guidebooks such as *Minitab* (Ryan and Joiner, 1985), which includes a special program that can be learned in short order and used from an "interactive" terminal. In addition, there is the Statistical Package for the Social Sciences (SPSS). See especially *SPSS Introductory Guide: Basic Statistics and Operations* (Norusis, 1982), *The SPSS Guide to Data Analysis* (Norusis, 1988),

SPSS Primer (Klecka, Norusis, and Hull, 1982), and *SPSS X: A Complete Guide to SPSS Language and Operations* (SPSS, Inc., 1983).

Your first step should be to purchase a good word-processing program in its *latest* edition. At this writing Macwrite, Word, WordPerfect, Wordstar, and WriteNow are five widely used programs. The one to choose will depend on both the kind of computer you have and the kinds of features your dissertation will require. For example, if your dissertation will include many mathematical formulas, tables, figures, charts, and other complex presentations, look for special formatting programs such as LATEX and Harvard Graphics. Even if you do not need the more powerful (and expensive) word-processing software, be sure to choose a program that will at least prepare footnotes, check for spelling and grammatical errors, and function as a thesaurus. Most of the major word-processing software companies have telephone numbers you can call (some are toll free) if you need help. As you know, printers can be attached to most microcomputers; so the machine can be used as a kind of super typewriter to prepare rough drafts of the thesis and make manuscript revisions. If the printer prepares letter-quality pages, the computer can be used to type the final draft of the thesis with proper margins and consecutively numbered pages. If it is attached to a laser printer, it can also produce high-quality charts, tables, graphs, maps, and much more. Although refinements in the next few years will make the microcomputer an even more valuable ally of the serious scholar, human imagination will still be required to deal with the most difficult and interesting scholarly questions.

Next, learn to do "online" database searches. You might start by purchasing or borrowing a modem for your home computer with which to search your university's online library holdings. Nowadays many libraries are set up for such searches, although what is online may be limited to the more recent books and periodicals. A modem will also be necessary if you want to call up your university's mainframe computer to analyze data or send and receive electronic mail.

If you have not already learned to do so, practice using the

CD-ROM (Compact Disk–Read Only Memory) facilities in your university library. Both for practice and just for the fun of it, search the CD-ROM *Dissertation Abstracts International (DAI)* on some topic of special interest. Later, when you begin to get serious about dissertation topics, you will need to search the *DAI* in earnest; it is wise, therefore, to become familiar with that priceless resource as soon as possible. (*Dissertation Abstracts International* and its companion computerized dissertation search facility, as well as other databased computer services, are discussed further in Chapters Three and Six.)

After you master the fundamentals, create a personal computer database in which you record information such as author, title, publisher, date, conclusions, and summaries of the important books, articles, monographs, papers, and dissertations you read. Commercial software packages are available for such purposes. Available, too, is software that performs sophisticated statistical analysis, although many students will continue to use the university mainframe for more complicated procedures. In any event, before you purchase anything, try it out. "Try before you buy" is an excellent maxim to remember when acquiring computer software or hardware. Fortunately, most universities have computer facilities and display rooms, where many of the programs (software) and the machines (hardware) on which to run the programs are available for your inspection and trial.

Finally, with your modem active explore the possibilities of communicating with the university's main computer, or mainframe. You may be able to use the university's sophisticated statistical analysis packages, plotting devices, graphics software, library search facilities, and more, all the while sitting at home or in your office. Investigate the possibility of communicating with other computer owners by means of campus computer bulletin boards and electronic mail (E-mail). You might even go international through LISTSERV, a worldwide message-distribution network. Some students send preliminary chapters of their dissertations to their advisers for comment.

It is true that computers have already changed many rudiments of thesis work; it is also true that what is written about them, including what is written here, will be obsolete within a few months. Nevertheless, certain adages endure. Every year computers are more reliable, but they do "crash" occasionally. As you work, therefore, always keep a second, or backup, disk as a copy in case your primary disk is damaged or destroyed. Some authorities recommend that all work should be backed up with two disks or tapes. For added insurance, print a "hard copy" of your work as it progresses and store it in a safe place.

Remember that in your search for books, periodicals, and other references, you cannot rely totally on databases; many of them go back only twenty-five or thirty years, and important sources can be overlooked despite your use of highly imaginative key-word descriptors. There is still no substitute for digging through the library's standard references in search of sources.

Be certain at the outset that you know what you want your computer to do. If you intend to perform some form of statistical analysis, you must understand the strengths and weaknesses of that particular form of analysis. Fortunately, a number of different statistical software packages are available, with suggestions on how to choose an appropriate analytical mode, enter data, find additional references, and more. Three of the most widely used are BMDP (Biomedical Data Programs), SPSS (Statistical Package for the Social Sciences), and SAS (Statistical Analysis System). Although these packages are readily available and people in your academic computing center can advise you on their use, it is your responsibility to know what you are doing.

2

Working with
the Research Adviser
and Advisory Committee

The choice of the research adviser is a vital one. As the Council of Graduate Schools (1990b, p.1) has pointed out, "A peculiarly close relationship exists between the research student and supervisor. They start as master and pupil and ideally end up as colleagues." Heiss (1970, p. 151) has described this relationship in strong terms: "The quality and character of the relationship between the doctoral student and his major professor is unequivocally the most sensitive and crucial element in the doctoral experience." Jean E. Girves and Virginia Wemmerus identify *financial support* and the *link between student and adviser* as "critical aspects to the graduate school experience" (1988, p. 165). Several doctoral students who studied the experiences of graduate students have reached the same conclusion (Benkin, 1984). The redoubtable Henry Rosovsky, formerly dean of the Faculty of Arts and Science at Harvard University, puts it bluntly: "For future scholars, course performance is not a reliable indicator of long-term success. The thesis is of far greater significance. So, I am urging an especially careful choice when it comes to the dissertation guide — the *Doktorvater* [doctor-father] or surrogate parent" (1990, p. 152). The Council of Graduate schools (1991, p. 5) makes the following recommendations:

> New doctoral students should be advised to meet all prospective dissertation advisers and talk with other students in the

24

program about the attributes of various advisers. To facilitate this practice, departments should provide students with (1) an annually updated list of graduate students with their dissertation topics and the names of their advisers, and (2) a similar list of departmental members of the graduate faculty with information about their areas of research, selected references to their publications, and indication of their availability to supervise dissertations.

Writing a doctoral dissertation or master's thesis is, undeniably, an emotional experience for all concerned—the student, his advisers, and everyone close to him. So seriously did one university department regard the selection of the adviser that it offered a required course aimed at ensuring that each incoming doctoral student had the "opportunity (and major responsibility) to choose his adviser carefully and at his own pace" (Lansbury, 1975, p. 511). Each student prepared for a series of interviews with faculty members by reading their published articles and monographs and writing reports on the work of three of them before choosing one as adviser. This process, although somewhat complex and certainly unconventional, testifies to the fact that the candidate should make every effort to find a research adviser who is knowledgeable, sympathetic, and yet demanding.

How are advisers appointed? On this matter practice varies; therefore, you would do well to learn the local ground rules as soon as possible. Some universities appoint an adviser as soon as a student is admitted for graduate study, and that person continues as adviser until the degree is awarded; some departments have one person serve as adviser to *all* graduate students until a dissertation sponsor (or supervisor) is appointed. Other departments assume that each graduate student will seek a faculty member as an informal adviser and that, when the time comes to write the dissertation, the informal adviser will offer to serve as the student's sponsor or mentor. My own experience was somewhat different. A professor I admired served as my unofficial adviser during the period of my course work and later as a member of my supervisory committee. However, because I chose a dissertation topic that was not within the sphere of his special competence, I was obliged to persuade another person to serve as the head of my dissertation committee.

How does one find the right adviser? If you have the opportunity to choose your adviser, select someone who has your respect as well as the trust and respect of his or her colleagues. As head of the dissertation committee, your adviser is in a position to influence the committee members on your behalf, but they will be influenced only if they regard your adviser as someone on whom others can rely. It goes without saying that you want an adviser with whom you can work comfortably, but the irony is that you also want your adviser to be tough enough to bring forth your best efforts. Of course, you will go partly on instinct in such matters, but graduate students do share opinions on the characteristics of the faculty, and, as a result, some professors are more in demand than others. The opinions of others are important; however, there is no substitute for acquiring a first-hand knowledge of the professors on a faculty by reading what they write and taking their classes. One should not assume that only the popular lecturers will qualify as knowledgeable and humane advisers. The less flamboyant professor may have the exciting ideas and—what is every bit as important—the ability to listen to students' ideas.

Robert Smith (1990) has some excellent advice for students in the sciences, advice probably applicable elsewhere as well. He describes three general types of advisers—the "collaborator type," the "hands-off type," and the "senior scientist type"—and notes the advantages and disadvantages of each. The "collaborator types," for example, may be younger scholars who are "keen to have their students achieve quick results" (p. 26). Because they are seeking promotion and tenure, they may be interested in joint publication. The "hands-off" advisers may be at mid-career and therefore somewhat less interested in quick results; on the other hand, they may allow a student more time than necessary to finish the dissertation. However, they may also provide good counsel. "Senior scientist" types are well along in their careers and thus able to provide experienced advice. If the senior scientist is a gifted researcher, the young advisee may become part of a priceless master-student relationship. But there is the danger that if scholarship has outdistanced an older scholar, the student may acquire outdated research skills (pp. 26–27). Young professors armed with the latest scholarly ideas and tools can be especially helpful, but they "may also be the most demanding" (p. 41). Should you change advisers if things do not seem to be working out? Smith thinks you should; in fact, your adviser may support your decision.

How are doctoral committees assembled, and how large are such committees? Here, too, practice varies, although the committees usually are composed of at least three members. Some universities rely on the recommendations of research advisers for the composition of committees. In others the department head will take work load and other factors into consideration in making appointments. Usually, however, the student will be able to influence the makeup of the committee. And, of course, the dissertation topic itself will be of prime importance in determining who will serve on the committee; those members of the faculty who are most knowledgeable about the area under study will be considered first. Sometimes a highly informed member of the faculty cannot be a member of your committee. In my own case, a professor who really should have been on my committee was away on a sabbatical leave and, as a result, did not serve. However, he returned just in time to be present at the final oral examination and, to my great relief, expressed support for what I had tried to do.

Just as practice varies on the method by which advisers and committees are chosen, so, too, advisers and committees have differing views of their roles. "Some believe that the student is more or less on his own. [Others] ride herd on the candidate on every point" (Heiss, 1970, p. 221). Student expectations vary as well. Some assume that the adviser will set objectives, assign research topics, and monitor progress. Others expect the adviser to play a minor role; as one student said, "The adviser should try to stay out of the way."

One should bear in mind the problem the committee members face in reconciling their dual role of guiding research and assessing the quality of the finished product. This is no easy task, as anyone who has ever tried to do it will testify. Each graduate student really should have two committees: one to give advice and another to evaluate the quality of the results. But imagine the hurt feelings, recriminations, and general mayhem that would result in a department if this practice were followed—not to mention all the committee meetings that would be necessary! Ideally, every member of the committee should be qualified both to advise the student and to judge the quality of the student's work; the research adviser should be the most highly qualified of all.

Sometimes it is wise to have a research specialist of some kind on your committee. If your study requires complex statistical techniques, for example, you may want your committee to include a faculty member who teaches your department's courses on statistics and research design. Needless to say, such persons are extremely important to the department and are sometimes overburdened with committee assignments. Even if they do not serve on your committee, such departmental specialists often prove invaluable to you when you plan your analytical approach to the data.

You will want a harmonious committee. Your research adviser will often be more aware than you are of the petty feuds and personality conflicts that bedevil many departments in the modern university. If two professors are constantly at loggerheads, it makes no sense to put them on the same dissertation committee. However, you do not necessarily want only the sweetness-and-light types. Many professors have the ability to work with colleagues even when they disagree on important scholarly questions; in fact, they take pleasure in differences of opinion. These wise men and women are to be found on most doctoral dissertation committees, and they are an asset, not a liability. They know how difficult and rewarding scholarship can be and are willing to help you discover the satisfaction that scholarship can give.

Should the relationship between student and adviser be closer than it is? In a study some years ago, Berelson (1960, p. 179) reported that 80 percent of all graduate faculty and recent recipients of the Ph.D. degree were satisfied with the closeness of the relationship. In the matter of direction and advice, Heiss (1970, p. 153) found that most of the 3,000 graduate students she studied were satisfied with their relationship with their thesis adviser; however, 6 percent reported that advisers gave too much direction, and 28 percent said they gave too little. It is, unquestionably, a difficult balance to strike. Of additional interest, by the way, is the fact that 82 percent reported that their advisers expected the candidate to take the initiative in arranging meetings to discuss matters of concern.

Occasionally, a problem arising between adviser and advisee stems, oddly enough, from excessive good manners and reticence on the part of a student. One manifestation of this condition was expressed as follows: "In working on my dissertation, I needed help far more often than I sought it. I hated to impose on busy professors whose role as adviser was only peripheral to their many obligations" (Tronsgard, 1963, p. 495). This student labored under a misapprehension: advising doctoral students on dissertations is certainly not a "peripheral" obligation of the research adviser, and no student need be inhibited on that score. Sometimes, however, a failure to seek advice may be motivated more by a reluctance to create an impression of ignorance. While this fear is understandable, a failure to seek advice may create the opposite impression equally damaging—that of insensitivity to the need for counsel. If, on occasion, an adviser seems to be doling out information that the student already knows, the student should take heart; the adviser has probably learned through hard experience that it is only too easy to overestimate how much students know— even the most advanced students. Most advisers give the same advice many times over the years until they have the uneasy feeling they are repeating themselves. Frequently they are, whereupon they stop giving advice and assume that all their advisees know everything they are supposed to know. Holmes (1976, p. 74) has excellent advice for anyone writing a book: "Never underestimate the intelligence of a reader, and never overestimate his knowledge." The same advice, suitably modified, might be tendered every adviser.

Below are a few more suggestions for dealing with the research adviser and committee:

As soon as possible, learn the mechanics of adviser and committee assignment. Since practice varies on this important point, you must learn the local ground rules as soon as possible. How are advisers chosen? When? How are committees constituted? What influence has the student over the membership of the advisory committee? How large is the committee? Is there representation from outside the department? Outside the university? What is the role of the adviser? The committee? Who conducts the defense of the dissertation? Is it the advisory committee? Who is the head of the advisory committee? Who is the head of the committee that conducts the final defense of the dissertation? What happens if the adviser or a member of the committee leaves the university?

Make notes of all meetings with the adviser and members of the research committee when the advice is still fresh in your mind. As already noted, most students are expected to initiate meetings at which advice and counsel are sought.

Ask your adviser whether you should submit a prospectus before preparing the formal dissertation proposal. Some advisers are satisfied to discuss an idea for a dissertation proposal before the formal proposal itself is drafted. Others like to see a prospectus, or preliminary paper, in which the idea for the dissertation is set forth, the research question cast, and the research procedure and analysis summarized. When the adviser is satisfied with the prospectus, you can then draft a full-scale proposal for consideration by the advisory committee.

Seek the advice of individual members of the committee. This suggestion may seem obvious, yet some graduate students seldom have much to do with anyone on their committee except the head of that committee or the research adviser.

Keep an eye on the committee. Sabbatical leaves have been known to remove professors from campus at times when their advisees needed them most. But do not be too upset if a member of the committee must be away or leaves the campus altogether. A substitute can usually be found to fill in.

Keep the committee informed of progress. This might be nothing more, for example, than a simple note to say you are off to New York to work in the public library for a few days.

Resist the impulse to give the committee members rough copy or first drafts. Even if "only a preliminary" opinion is sought, always submit pages on which serious labor has been expended. If you give them material that is obviously rough, they may think you are not really serious about your idea.

Give the committee time to read the manuscript. Often members of committees are presented with long papers on Tuesday and told that an opinion is desperately needed by Thursday. It goes without saying that this sort of thing cuts two ways: sometimes committee members are guilty of misplacing proposals given for study, forgetting appointments, and the like.

Ask your adviser whether you should submit the dissertation chapter by chapter or as a whole. Some advisers prefer to see each chapter as it is completed. Some prefer to see only a good draft of the whole dissertation; having read it, they return it for more work and polishing. The committee members, moreover, may have their own preferences; some, for example, want to see the whole dissertation, but only after the research adviser has had a chance to offer suggestions for improvement; others like to see a chapter at a time. This matter is rather quickly and easily resolved if a few inquiries are made ahead of time.

Be aware of graduate school deadlines for final examinations, final typed copies, and the like. Many advisers do not have all these administrative details at their fingertips, nor should they; but they will be of keen interest to you if you plan to march at a specific convocation to accept the doctoral hood or master's diploma.

3

Selecting and Shaping
the Research Topic

A colleague at the University of California, Berkeley, maintains that students seeking a thesis topic must first steep themselves in the literature of their field. Only then will they be prepared to recognize a fruitful idea when they encounter it. A single provocative passage in a book can set the creative process in motion; an experimental finding reported in a professional journal may suggest further research that can be profitably pursued in a dissertation project. Literally thousands of ideas await the student who is capable of imaginative thought and hard, determined inquiry.

Suggestions from others — research advisers, faculty members, fellow students — can also point to intriguing thesis possibilities. A research adviser may outline several rewarding areas for investigation, one of which will seize your imagination. Or as a member of a research team, you may choose to pursue a particular line of inquiry that will advance the work of the whole team. This latter approach is more common in the biological and physical sciences than in the humanities or social sciences (Berelson, 1960, p. 178). Perhaps many disciplines could benefit from ideas engendered by such team endeavors; on the other hand, there is much to be said for the lonely scholar working under solitary conditions on a problem of keen personal interest.

When should the search for a dissertation topic begin? Berelson (p. 180) found that about half of all students do not begin to look for a topic until after they have passed the qualify-ing (or general) examination. Perhaps the best advice is to start the serious search for a subject as soon as doctoral study begins. With the thesis topic in hand early in the graduate experience, you can select courses and write papers that will provide a sturdy base of academic support for the projected research.

There is no need to be compulsive at this initial stage; rather, keep the eyes open and the mind alert and receptive to promising ideas. Some authorities suggest starting a disserta-tion topic file in which to keep track of ideas that seem worthy of pursuit (Davis and Parker, 1979, p. 23). In many cases an idea that translates into a substantial dissertation will also lead to other ideas that can be productively explored over a lifetime of serious scholarship.

Where to Look

Here are some specific suggestions for tracking down the elusive dissertation topic. Visit the library to find copies of recent dissertations in appropriate fields of study. Because you want your models to be the best obtainable, try to find dissertations that have won awards; professional associations sometimes rec-ognize superior theses, and so do some departments and schools. Also, ask your adviser to recommend any especially praiseworthy efforts. When you find good dissertations, read them to see whether the authors make suggestions for further research; often several writers in a field of study will mention the same problems as worthy of further scholarship.

Check the professional journals. Some of them publish lists of "dissertations completed" and "dissertations under way." Such lists will indicate what scholars at other universities think is important in your field and will help you recognize what part of the field is still unexplored. Furthermore, when you have selected your topic, you will know the names of those at work on topics related to your own.

If the graduate students in your department get together from time to time to discuss proposals for research before submitting them to faculty committees, attend such a session; if none exists, organize one. Some graduate students' associations, in cooperation with the university's graduate school, publish lists of dissertations under way. These can be invaluable sources to put you in touch with work progressing in your own department and in other departments of your university as well.

Study articles in recent issues of your professional journals to learn what topics are of high current interest and promise to remain so for a few years to come. This is tricky; still, if something is drawing the attention of the best scholars in your field and if it seems interesting, why not pursue it?

Ask the librarians to run a database search on some topic of interest. It is surprising what information is to be found in the dozens of databases now in service. A database search may even turn up a list of recently completed dissertations in a given field. One such search provided the following: "This bibliography represents a compilation of Agriculture and Agronomy doctoral research for 1971–1979. Each of the 3,386 doctoral dissertations cited herein has been accepted by accredited degree-granting universities in North America." (For more information on databases, see the section headed "Computer-Based Reference Services" in Chapter Six.)

With an idea for a topic in mind, search for other dissertations already written on the same general subject. In view of the stipulation on originality in thesis research, you must determine whether your study will duplicate an existing one. If you find that it does, you must propose an original approach to your topic or abandon it in favor of a new one. Even if you find that no one has studied your proposed topic, it is still probable that at least one person has written a dissertation on a subject closely enough related to be of keen interest to you. You will wish to obtain any such dissertations for close study. As mentioned in Chapter One, a prime source of such information is *Dissertation Abstracts International (DAI)*, a service of University Microfilms International in Ann Arbor, Michigan. Manuscripts can be ordered in photocopy form, slightly reduced in size, or on microfiche or microfilm. There is, of course, a charge for this service. Fortunately, *Dissertation Abstracts International* is in CD-ROM disk form available for searches on a self-service basis. Or, for a fee, a library specialist in the use of computers will search the *DAI* and provide a computer-printed list of the results. Some of the information will be useless; some will turn out to be pure gold.

Before you begin a search of titles and abstracts related to your topic, however, draw up a list of key words or combinations of words and phrases you might expect to encounter. This list can be broadened or refined as you proceed. For helpful suggestions consult the *Library of Congress — Subject Headings* (1988) or look at the key words in the guides to the databases. When your search is over, you should have an answer to the question "Would a doctoral dissertation on this topic be possible?" If this preliminary search has uncovered a dissertation on the general topic you propose to investigate, your answer will have to be a qualified "Perhaps, if I propose something important and original on this topic." And, if you are serious about pursuing this topic further, you might want to have a discussion with your adviser on what qualifies as *original* and *important*. In any event, when your proposal is discussed, be prepared for your adviser and members of the supervisory committee to ask, "Have any other dissertations been written on this topic?" Your answer, if you have done your library work: "I have searched the *DAI* and found that no one has done what I propose to do." You might also have to add: "I did find six dissertations on topics related to mine. Nevertheless, I believe that I can make an original contribution to an understanding of this topic."

Criteria to Keep in Mind

Once you have come up with a promising idea, you must subject it to careful scrutiny to determine whether it meets the following criteria:

1. It must *sustain your interest* and stimulate your imagination, so that you will bring to bear upon it your full creative abilities.
2. It must be *within your range of competence*.
3. It must be *manageable* in size.

4. It must have the potential to make *an original contribution* to human knowledge. (Discussion of this criterion was begun in Chapter One.)
5. It must be based on *obtainable* data.
6. It must permit you to *demonstrate your independent mastery* of both the subject and the appropriate research method.

When you have settled these matters to your satisfaction, you may want to ask yourself four additional questions: Is there a theory or theories that bear in some way upon my idea? (For further discussion of theory, see the section in Chapter Four entitled "Review of Relevant Research and Theory.") Are there faculty members in my department who might have an interest in this topic? Does this topic have future research possibilities? What will leading scholars in my field think of this topic?

Manageable Size. Certainly, the dimensions of the topic are vitally important. Most doctoral candidates—and master's candidates, too, for that matter—begin with a topic that is too large to be handled successfully. Early in the selection process, it is wise to try to assess the amount of time you will need to complete the thesis. If a biographical study is contemplated, you may be well advised to exercise caution. A biography of Andrew Carnegie, or one of George Eliot, is probably too ambitious for a dissertation. But even a biography of someone less well known presents problems, because biographical studies can be particularly time-consuming, as anyone who has undertaken to write one will attest. Years of painstaking effort may be required to do justice to the subject and the resources available. Give up on a biography, then? Not necessarily. But it may be wise to limit the dissertation to an important segment of the subject's life or work, with a vow to undertake a full-scale biography after the degree has been awarded. You might study, for example, the influence of Andrew Carnegie's benefactions on American public libraries at the turn of the century. Such a topic may still be broad, but it certainly is much more manageable than a full-scale biography of the steelmaker. Or assume that you have become interested in George Eliot but decide that a full-scale biography is out of the question, whereas an appraisal of Spinoza's philosophy as an influence on Eliot's writing is both intriguing and manageable.

On the length of completed dissertations, studies reveal a wide variation. The 600 dissertations examined by Davis and Parker (1979, p. 15) ranged from fewer than 100 to more than 600 pages, with a median length of 225 pages. Berelson (1960, p. 181) found the following variations in average page totals: physical sciences, 105; biological sciences, 108; professional fields, 171; social sciences, 226; humanities, 285. The amount of time needed to complete the task also varies. Davis and Parker's estimate is somewhere between a year and a half to three years (p. 17). Some universities place a five-year limit on the interval between the general or qualifying examination and the completion of the dissertation.

A number of authorities favor relatively short dissertations (Spurr, 1970, p. 133). Barzun (1968, p. 36) maintains that "life-sentence" dissertations are fast disappearing. Research advisers nowadays are swamped with work and tend to view "with lack-luster eye the student who has chosen to tell all in twelve hundred typed pages." Again, the adviser and committee members are charged with keeping projects within reasonable limits.

Your Range of Competence. As for your competence to take on a particular study, it is obvious that you must know or be prepared to learn the skills that will be needed. If you write about Carnegie and the public libraries, you will need to learn a good deal about public libraries at the turn of the century; if you plan to investigate the elements of Spinoza's philosophy in Eliot's work, you will need some background in metaphysics and solid grounding in the complicated philosophy of Spinoza. Don't be discouraged; your university has courses on such matters, and, even more important, there are books on these subjects.

If you undertake a documentary study, you must have some familiarity with documentary research techniques. Helpful here are courses in historiography or in the historical period under study. Similarly, dissertations in the behavorial sciences will demand knowledge of specialized behavioral research techniques. Many areas will require a combination of skills; all demand literary proficiency. When more than one research skill is called for, you must be sure you are highly competent in the major skill needed and at least adequate in the others.

On occasion a student will come up with a topic that seems ideal, only to have it rejected by the committee. Should this be your experience, you must find out the reasons for rejection and make a fresh start. In the long run, you will usually find that the committee has done you a favor. Scrapping a topic and starting anew is not unusual at this stage. Indeed, fully one-third of all successful candidates actually began more than one dissertation topic.

The disappointed candidate may ask, "Is only one kind of topic acceptable? Is one approach preferred over others? Is the statistical (or experimental, or ethnographic, or historical) study the only acceptable one in my field?" Unfortunately, there are fashions in dissertation topics just as in hemlines. Furthermore, some departments and institutions regard only certain research methods as legitimate and reject topics that propose to utilize methods accepted in other disciplines. Such severe limitations on research technique must be deplored when the result is to cut the candidate off from the contributions of scholars in related fields.

Originality. Early in the selection process, you will have to come to grips with the question of what qualifies as "an original contribution to knowledge." The answer is not easy, for scholarly opinion — inevitably, perhaps — differs. Originality is not always readily recognizable, nor is it always accepted as such. Basically, however, a topic must have the potential to do at least one of the following: uncover new facts or principles, suggest relationships that were previously unrecognized, challenge existing truths or assumptions, afford new insights into little-understood phenomena, or suggest new interpretations of known facts that can alter people's perceptions of the world around them.

Fortunately, there are a few steps a student can take toward identifying an appropriate topic, always bearing in mind that the research adviser and the other members of the dissertation committee will have to approve the selected topic.

A good place to begin is with these questions: "Are the facts or evidence on which I shall rely old? New? A little of both?" "Are my findings or conclusions likely to add new and important facts to the sum of human knowledge?" Obviously, if the answer is "old" to the first question and "no" to the second, then it is unlikely that anything particularly original will be forthcoming. But if the answer is "new," at least in the main, and if something significant promises to emerge from your research, then you may indeed expect your dissertation to qualify as an original contribution to knowledge.

Of course, there is always the question of degree: just *how original* must that contribution be? Will a fresh, innovative research technique yield truly original results? Not necessarily. Once again, the committee and research adviser will have to provide the answer. Occasionally a student will propose an intensive survey of the literature of a particular field. As a rule, this type of study will not make a legitimate dissertation; yet now and again someone will come up with an approach that upsets this dictum. What about a topic that promises a fresh, innovative look at old theories, established facts, entrenched institutions? The answer, of course, will have to depend on the anticipated outcomes. Mere description of what you see from a new vantage point may not elicit any significant new information or insights. But drawing conclusions that shed some light on a previously murky area of understanding is another matter entirely.

Consider a dissertation entitled "Income Distribution in the United States in 1990." Would this topic be acceptable to an advisory committee? With only the title to go on and other considerations aside, the answer is "probably not," because the title seems to indicate that the results would be little more than a list of facts or a collection of data; indeed, the research required to complete such a study is most properly accomplished under the aegis of some governmental agency concerned with income distribution statistics. Consequently, topics of this nature usually are not encouraged by research committees. On the other hand, they may be inclined to look with at least some degree of favor on a study that envisions an analysis of data available from governmental sources — perhaps a question similar to the following: "Have certain advances in medical technology influenced income distribution within the medical professions?"

Independent Mastery. Not only must the dissertation plow new intellectual ground; it should also represent an independent contribution to knowledge. Members of doctoral committees rightly assume that the thesis will be the fruit of your labor and no one else's. You may, of course, seek and receive advice; providing such assistance is, after all, one of the prime duties of the research adviser and the committee. The final product, however, should be primarily your own work, even when you have been involved in a collaborative study.

In its policy statement on joint authorship, the Council of Graduate Schools (1990a, pp. 24–25) has attempted to clarify what can be a complicated situation: "Many universities explicitly state that the doctoral dissertation must be the work of a single author, i.e., joint or co-authored dissertations are not acceptable." Nonetheless, the council makes this concession: "However, recognizing the frequency of collaborative and team efforts in present day research, some institutions specify conditions under which collaborative research may be acceptable for doctoral dissertations." The "conditions" might include, for example, a statement detailing precisely what the candidate contributed to the whole as well as an assertion that the major part of the dissertation is the work of the candidate.

The Search for Relationships

Assume that you have an idea for a dissertation topic — one that seems to meet the criteria set forth earlier in this chapter. You may still need to shape or focus your topic before writing the formal dissertation proposal; and the best way I know to shape or focus a topic is to draft a research question (and accompanying subsidiary questions or hypotheses) in which you seek to determine the "relationship" between two or more variables, concepts, phenomena, events, or things. In the section just ahead, you will find examples of research questions, but before we turn to those examples, it is important for us to consider the word *relationship*, which is often the key term of a powerful research question, even if only implied.

How many terms are there, you may ask, that imply relationship? A good many. When you draft your research proposal, no matter what your field of study, you may wish to consider one or more of the following as the term or terms expressing relationship in your research question: *affect, affinity, analogous, ancillary, approximate, associate, cause, compare, compatible, concomitant, connect, consecutive, consistent, continuous, correspond, counterpart, depend, different, divergent, effect, embed, equal, equivalent, greater, homogeneity, homologous, identical, independent, indicate, influence, less, like, link, near, opposite, parallel, pattern, peripheral, proportional, reciprocate, reflect, regular, relate, similar, subordinate, superordinate, symmetrical, tension,* and *unlike*.

To learn how often each of these words (and fifty-three others) appeared in dissertation titles and abstracts, I searched *Dissertation Abstracts International* from January 1989 to June 1990. Some of the most frequently used words that emerged were *effect, different, associate, influence, similar, less, pattern, greater, dependent, regular,* and *affect*. The word *relationship* appeared 14,285 times, making it the third most frequently used. I then checked to see how many dissertation abstracts used five of the more frequently used words: *effect, different, influence, similar,* and *pattern*. Eighteen abstracts used all five words at least once, and one used the five words a total of twenty-two times. Words such as these indicate relationships that serve as the bedrock for research questions. (Incidentally, using a computer equipped with a CD-ROM for the *Dissertation Abstracts International*, I turned up these word frequencies in less than three hours.)

Perhaps the most daring and evocative word ever used to express a relationship is *cause*. It can be the source of both ecstasy and despair for the researcher. How often has a high correlation between two variables seduced the investigator into assuming a cause-and-effect relationship, only to have this comfortable assumption dashed by the realization that a third variable was responsible? "If when the tide is falling you take out water with a twopenny pail, you and the moon can do a great deal" (Beveridge, 1951, p. 20). Some scholars contend that the word *cause* should never be used: "In the mid-eighteenth century, the philosopher David Hume showed that the conception of Cause as a compelling push that produces an effect is an illusion. . . . All that is agreed upon is that where Cause is, there is Regularity" (Barzun and Graff, 1985, p. 186). "The ultimate question for the historian therefore is: What pattern?" (p. 191).

In many disciplines the two basic methods of determining whether a relationship exists are (1) experimental procedures and (2) correlational studies. Sometimes a combination of both methods is needed, especially when the circumstances make it impossible to gather experimental evidence to the degree that will satisfy the scholarly purist. The continuing dispute over the effects of cigarette smoking as a cause of lung cancer is a case in point.

One of the primary grounds for challenging the contention that heavy smoking is a probable cause of lung cancer is that most of the evidence is correlational in nature. That is to say, the incidence of lung cancer is significantly higher among heavy smokers than it is among nonsmokers; from this fact it is inferred that heavy smoking probably causes lung cancer or, at any rate, contributes to the conditions that foster it.

Now, ideally, when a high correlation of this kind is found, a carefully controlled experiment will be conducted in which the independent variable — in this instance, smoking — is manipulated, and all other variables are strictly controlled. (Of course, under this experimental procedure, the dependent variable — lung cancer — would be carefully diagnosed.) At the end of the experiment, it will be seen whether the finding suggested by the correlational study is borne out by the evidence; to wit, that the heavy smoking does, in fact, lead to lung cancer. If the experiment bears out what was implied by the correlational study, the conclusion is that smoking causes lung cancer. The correlational study — in this instance, at least — *suggested* the possibility of a causal relationship between smoking and cancer, but it was the experiment that permitted confidence in the discovery of a causal relationship. Many scholars insist that the correlational study can *never* establish a causal relationship; that only a true experiment with all variables carefully controlled can supply the answers. Other scholars insist that the word *cause* should never be used in the discussion of scholarly findings, because all findings must forever be regarded as tentative and, therefore, open to refutation. Perhaps they are correct.

Obviously, the cancer-smoking controversy cannot at present be resolved by experimental procedures in which *all* variables are held constant. To learn whether smoking causes lung cancer, investigators would have to work with two groups of infants—identical twins—regulating their lives in every way and eventually inducing one group to smoke and the other to refrain. A fifty- or sixty-year period would have to elapse before all the evidence would be in on the incidence of cancer in the smoker group. Feasible? No. Ridiculous? Perhaps. But some such procedure would be necessary if purely experimental evidence is demanded to satisfy the requirements of the deepest scholarly craving. Experiments with rats or primates would not be entirely acceptable, for rats and primates are not humans. Even studies of human subjects present obstacles. For example, a convent might seem a likely place to find a reliable group of nonsmokers. But nuns are not male; and even a comparison with female smokers might raise some scientific hackles, since the nuns' religious orientation might suggest still another set of variables not taken into consideration. And how does one take into account the fact that nonsmokers also contract lung cancer?

If experimental evidence is not available, what is the scholar to do? The answer is obvious: make the best of what is available. Perhaps, as with the research into the cause of lung cancer, careful correlational studies and modest experimental procedures will have to suffice until someone can devise more rigorous experimental procedures to overcome the objections to anything less than a longitudinal study spanning half a century. In the meantime, the *predictive* relationships can continue to be a guide to action. It is highly probable, for example, that a person who steps in front of a speeding truck will be injured or even killed. Very likely he will not need to be convinced of a causal relationship by experimental means; a predictive relationship will suffice to keep him on the curb. Similarly, a heavy smoker who is made aware of the probable consequences of smoking may be induced to abstain whether or not he is convinced of a causal relationship.

You should not, of course, settle for correlational evidence when the experimental evidence can be obtained; but neither should you feel that you must apologize for your research when it is not of the experimental variety. Correlational studies can be both productive and worthwhile when done with care and restraint; in certain disciplines they will have to be relied on for the foreseeable future and probably forever. The historian, for example, must use a nonexperimental approach because she cannot re-create the personalities, events, and conditions that combined to produce historical record. Barring the miracle of a device that will enable her to return to the past, the historian must seek to determine the relationships between persons and events by studying documents, books, reports, films, and a host of other sources; she will continue to forge questions to ask, to draft theories by which to conduct her research, and to improve the generalizations she has advanced.

Finally, something must be said about the role of chance in discovery—not the statistician's chance, or unexplained variance, as important as that is; rather, the good luck or serendipitous results that are sometimes more important than the findings the scholar pursues. "Probably the majority of discoveries in biology and medicine," Beveridge (1951, p. 31) insists, "have been come upon unexpectedly, or at least had an element of chance in them, especially the most important and revolutionary ones." An exaggeration? Perhaps. Nonetheless, one of the chief delights of every serious scholar comes from the enchanting lures of scholarship and the fact that from time to time someone is privileged to solve a mystery—even if it is a mystery he did not intend to solve.

Research Question, Definitions of Terms, Subsidiary Questions

When you have determined to your satisfaction that the possibility of a relationship exists between the variables, concepts, phenomena, events, or things in your dissertation topic, your next step is to formulate a research question. Assume you have chosen *influence* as your term of relationship; how does your question now read? "What influence has *A* on *B*?" "What influence has *B* on *A*?" "Is the influence of the two variables *A* and *B* reciprocal?" "If *A* is changed slightly, will there be a concomitant change in the influence of *A* on *B*?" "What happens to the influence of *A* on *B* if one or more additional factors are introduced?" These and other such questions will suggest themselves until you hit on just the right way to phrase the question.

Although a good research question may appear to be reducible to a few seemingly simple parts, the actual process of its formulation is anything but simple. Rather, it is the product of the most vigorous intellectual effort and may, in fact, be regarded as the quintessence of scholarship. To illustrate how the research question may be stated, I have gathered together a number of actual dissertation titles or subjects, along with other scholarly writings. Look carefully at each example to determine how well it meets the definition of a research question. Does it contain a word that implies relationship? Does it contain at least two phenomena, concepts, variables, events, or things?

1. What was the influence of economic forces on the drafters of the United States Constitution?
2. What is the effect of a student's level of intelligence on his or her success in college?
3. In a dissertation written at Princeton, Raymond Baxter (1976) sought the "Effects of Institutionalization on the Social-Psychological Well-Being of the Aged."
4. How much did slavery, conflicting economic interests, differences in social structure and values, and political rivalries contribute to the start of the American Civil War?
5. What influence did the writings of Plato and Aristotle have on Thomas More's *Utopia*? (Thomas White, Columbia, 1974)
6. What factors in schools as they are currently organized in the United States contribute most to a child's educational experience? (Coleman, 1966)

7. "Plantation Management: Its Influence on Soil Fertility, Herbaceous Vegetation and Growth of Fraser Fir and Norway Spruce." (Stuart Lynn Warren, North Carolina State University, 1986)

8. "Molecular Oxygen as a Reagent in the Development of New Synthetic Methods." (Bruce Lipshutz, Yale, 1977)

9. "The Effects of Temperature and Salinity on the Phospholipid and Fatty Acid Composition of a Halotolerant, Psychrotolerant Bacterium Isolated from Antarctic Dry Valley Soil." (Karen Joy Miller, University of Massachusetts, 1984)

10. What are "The Sources of Variability in Juvenile Court Decision-Making"? (Curt Griffiths, Montana, 1977)

11. "Interaction of Calcium, Metal Ions, and Calmodulin Antagonist Drugs and Target Proteins with Calmodulin." (John Steven Mills, Ohio State University, 1987)

12. "The Use of Clinical, Laboratory, and Radiology Findings to Predict Admission, Need for Admission, and Surgery in Emergency Room Patients with Abdominal Pain." (Barbara Mary Langland, UCLA, 1987)

13. What are the "Effects of Suburban Growth Controls on Low- and Middle-Income Households in Metropolitan Regions"? (Joenathan Dean, Princeton, 1977)

14. "Trailing Edge Flow Conditions as a Factor in Airfoil Design." (Mark David Maughmer, University of Illinois, 1984)

15. "A Historical Investigation of the Impact of World War II on Harvard Medical School, 1938–1948." (Ilona Phyllis Swarz, University of Connecticut, 1983)

16. "Effects of Coumarin and Indanedione Anticoagulants on Prothrombin Synthesis and Vitamin-K Epoxide Cycle in Normal and Warfarin Resistant Rats." (Peter Ren, University of Rhode Island, 1976)

17. How would three prenatal psychological interventions affect the course and outcome of pregnancy? (Mary Dart, Harvard, 1977)

18. "The Impact of Presentence Investigation on Plea Bargained Dispositions in Kings County Supreme Court (New York)." (Joseph Enright, City University of New York, 1987)

19. Multivariate technique was used to study "Cranio-Vertebral Shape Changes in Man and Various Nonhuman Primates." (Robert Rondinelli, Illinois, 1977)
20. "Ability, Performance, and Compensation: A Theoretical and Empirical Investigation of Managerial Labor Contracts." (Kevin Murphy, University of Chicago, 1984)
21. "The Theater of His Glory: Nature and the Natural Order in the Thought of John Calvin." (Susan Elizabeth Schreiner, Duke University, 1983)
22. "A Study of Selected Psychological Factors Related to Completion or Non-completion of the Doctoral Dissertation Among Male and Female Doctoral Degree Applicants." (Toby Tesser Hobish, New York University, 1978)
23. "An Empirical Analysis of the Effects of State Usury Laws on the Performance of Savings and Loan Associations and Housing Starts in 1974." (James Proctor, Clemson, 1976)
24. "The genesis of this book," wrote Barbara W. Tuchman, "was a desire to find out what were the effects on society of the most lethal disaster of recorded history—that is to say, of the Black Death of 1348–50, which killed an estimated one third of the population living between India and Iceland." (*A Distant Mirror: The Calamitous Fourteenth Century*, 1978)

Many of the foregoing titles or subjects seek to define the relationship between two elements; another sampling might turn up more examples that encompass a multiplicity of factors, as reflected in such titles as "A Multivariate [or Systems, or Critical, or Stratificational] Analysis [of Data]." Some of these terms are familiar, others less so; but usually you can assume that the thesis so entitled has employed some sort of sophisticated analytical technique to elicit essential information on relationships. Still another version of the research question attempts to identify interactions among variables. As the research question increases in complexity, so do the data to be collected, and sometimes—although not always—the significance of the results obtained.

After the research question has been carefully stated,

each major word must be adequately defined. By way of example, consider a research question that asks how two major factors—intellectual potential and performance in high school—are related to success in college. The researcher will be expected, at the outset, to define the three key words in this question:

- *Intellectual potential*: A student's scores on the verbal and quantitative components of the Scholastic Aptitude Test.
- *Performance in high school*: Grade point average combined with an assessment of activities outside the classroom (such as singing in the chorus or editing the school paper).
- *Success in college*: Grade point average, length of stay in college, extracurricular activities, and the like.

The last task in the process of shaping or focusing the dissertation topic is to assemble the subsidiary questions. Both secondary and supplementary in nature, these questions will help to determine what data must be collected and to refine the complexity of the relationships that must be explored. They may even help to determine the methods of analysis that will be used. From the research question given above, the following subsidiary questions might emerge:

1. Do the verbal and quantitative scores on the Scholastic Aptitude Test (SAT) match the collegiate grade point average?
2. Does the grade point average in high school correspond with extracurricular activities in college?
3. How effectively do such factors as SAT scores, high school grade point average, and participation in high school activities—singly and in combination—predict whether a student will complete college?

One of the major advantages of working out the research and subsidiary questions with care is that they will often point to the proper methods of analysis. In the instance above, for example, multiple regression might be considered for part of the analysis; analysis of variance and other methods no doubt might also be employed.

Some advisers believe that if the inquiry is to have the precision it demands, the research question must be accompanied by carefully drafted hypotheses. Moreover, they may prefer a particular method for stating the hypotheses. One such form posits no significant difference between *A* and *B*; another predicts that *A* will be either significantly larger or smaller than *B*; a third form (more common perhaps) predicts the direction of the difference between *A* and *B*, as in the statement "When *A* increases, there will be significant increase in *B* as well." (Some scholars find the interaction between variables the most intriguing of all.)

Often the study itself determines the form the hypotheses will assume. If both empirical evidence and solid theory support it, for example, you might be wise to use the form of hypothesis that predicts the direction of a significant change in the dependent variable. Consider again the relationship between intellectual potential and performance in high school to success in college. Backed by supporting evidence and reputable theory, you might predict:

1. A significant positive correlation between the verbal score on the SAT and the collegiate grade point average.
2. A significant positive correlation between the high school grade point average and the number of extracurricular activities pursued in college.

As discussed in Chapter Four, the research question and subsidiary questions are major elements of the research proposal. Research, however, is seldom as straightforward as outlined here. For example, Chapter Four contains a section devoted to "Review of Relevant Research and Theory." Certainly, before a topic is selected and a research question posed, a scholar will conduct a preliminary review of relevant research and will consider any authoritative theories or explanations that bear directly on the topic. The research process does not always proceed from one step to the next. Rather, as in the case of topic selection, it frequently includes several intellectual activities that proceed simultaneously until a specific topic meets the appropriate criteria and is worthy of discussion with the research adviser and members of the supervisory committee.

4

Preparing
the Research Proposal

Let us assume that you have found an interesting topic — one that promises to be both significant and manageable; furthermore, after searching the usual reference collections, computer databases, *Dissertation Abstracts International*, and other resources, you are satisfied that the topic has not been the subject of another dissertation, monograph, or book. Although you may have come upon papers and books on closely related subjects, you are persuaded that your topic, properly presented, makes a fresh and significant contribution to the sum of human knowledge. Let us assume, also, that your adviser has expressed serious interest in what you propose to do and has encouraged you to proceed.

You are now ready to begin the next task: the preparation of the formal thesis or dissertation proposal. The research proposal is often the key element to the successful dissertation and, as such, the most important step in the whole process. An acceptable dissertation may conceivably be produced without this preliminary exercise; to omit it, however, is to court danger. Occasionally a student will insist that a close working relationship with her thesis adviser makes a formal proposal unnecessary. Perhaps — if all goes according to schedule. But what happens if the adviser leaves the university for another post before the dissertation is finished? Can the candidate hope to achieve the same level of mutual understanding with a new adviser? And what about the other members of the research committee? Without a formal proposal to spell out the details, can they be expected to understand exactly what the scholar intends to accomplish? Similarly, a student involved in a cooperative research project may feel that an individual thesis proposal would be redundant. Actually, the reverse is true. Even those institutions that accept theses based on collaborative research insist that a substantial portion of the completed manuscript be the candidate's own work. In such cases the formal proposal can be invaluable in defining the nature and extent of individual contributions to joint endeavors.

There are still other compelling reasons for writing a dissertation proposal even when it is not a hard-and-fast requirement. Most important, it forces the student to adopt a coherent, systematic procedure, which is essential to any scholarly enterprise. A methodical plan of attack outlined in a formal proposal will permit a greater degree of flexibility than will a superficial statement of purpose. Like the violinist who has mastered his technique and his instrument, the researcher who brings discipline and skills to her task will find the freedom and the confidence she needs to interpret, create, and improvise. Both have a tremendous advantage over those who pin their hopes on some mystical intuitive power that will enable them to "do what comes naturally."

There is no question that care lavished on the formal proposal will be repaid a thousand times. Moreover, work expended at this stage is never wasted, for much of the proposal can be incorporated into the final manuscript, either directly or with only slight modification.

The remainder of this chapter is devoted to a delineation of the elements of a proposal, followed by a discussion of each element with appropriate examples. (Two sample proposals will be found in the resource section at the back of the book.)

Although their form may vary, most dissertation proposals will comprise the following elements in a span of approximately twelve to thirty-two pages:

1. *The cover page*, which lists the proposed title; the author's name, address, and telephone number; the name of the institution; the degree sought; the names of the advisory members; and the date of submission.

2. *A one-page abstract*, usually written last but following the cover page in the proposal submitted to the committee. The device serves two purposes: it summarizes for the reader the basic structure of the proposal, and it refreshes the reader's memory on salient points in later discussions.

3. *A four-part statement of the research problem*, usually accomplished in four to fourteen pages, in the following order:

   a. *Introduction*, in which you state as succinctly as possible the nature of the problem as you perceive it, why you consider it important, and how you hope to contribute to its solution.

   b. *The research question* (or hypothesis), stated in the form of an interrogative sentence that asks the relationship between two or more concepts, variables, phenomena, events, things. Great care and thought should be given to phrasing this initial proposition, which will determine the thrust of your research efforts and point you firmly in the right direction (see also the discussion in Chapter Three).

   c. *Definitions of terms*, as discussed in Chapter Three.

   d. *Subsidiary questions* (or subhypotheses), which, like the research question, may be stated in hypothesis form.

   e. *Review of relevant research and theory.* Every researcher owes much to his predecessors and his contemporaries at work in the field or in libraries, laboratories, and studies. While it is both useful and appropriate to recognize their contributions, there is a noticeable tendency to drag in studies that have only the most tenuous connection with the research in hand. As a result, this section of the dissertation proposal sometimes has a disjointed quality or becomes a mere catalogue or listing of research with a bit of annotation added. This will not suffice. Required here is an integrated statement that affords some explanation of why the studies and theories cited are important to the work you propose to undertake.

4. *The procedure* (from four to fourteen pages), which may include:

a. *A description of the theoretical or conceptual framework to be employed.*
b. *Sources of evidence and authority.*
c. *Analytical technique and research design.*
d. *Timetable for completing the dissertation.*

Not surprisingly, the section on procedure is often the weakest part of the dissertation proposal. After all, many neo-phyte scholars have never produced a full-scale monograph or anything approaching it in content, rigor, or scope. They may have written innumerable term papers (many of them dashed off in the wee hours to meet an imminent deadline) or case studies or essays. A dissertation, however, is none of these. Properly executed, it should place you on some frontier of knowledge. Your area of expertise may be limited, but within this area you should be able to speak with genuine authority.

Moreover, a careful statement of procedure can be an invaluable guide for you; your research adviser; and other ex-perts, such as computer programmers, who will need to know precisely what is being attempted if they are to lend their exper-tise to the task.

The last item in the procedure element — the timetable for completing the dissertation — is a tentative schedule for each stage from the preliminary study to the presentation of final copies to members of the advisory committee.

5. *A trial table of contents* (one or two pages), which has three major advantages to recommend it: it indicates to the reader the dimensions of the topic; it affords the writer a temporary organizational framework; it helps to simplify the process of note taking.
6. *A brief bibliography* (one to five pages), which may be partially annotated. Its chief advantages are that it enables the ad-viser to form an opinion of the quality of the sources avail-able and to suggest any useful references the study may have overlooked. Work on a preliminary bibliography is time and energy well spent, for it is the foundation for the more

comprehensive listing that will accompany the finished dissertation.

Statement of Problem, Research Question, Subsidiary Questions

The foregoing pages set forth the raw elements of the proposal. The next step is to put the elements together to form an acceptable whole. Where to begin? There is much to be said for pondering the topic for a few days before attempting to think about the specific parts. How do you feel about the subject now that you are about to prepare a formal proposal? Is it still exciting to contemplate? What research might you undertake once you have finished this line of investigation? These and other questions come to mind. When you have begun to feel comfortable with your topic in its entirety, you can turn your attention to each element in order. If this bit of advice seems somewhat strange, consider it as an attempt to appreciate the forest before looking at the trees.

As you take up the specific elements, you will see how critical it is to have a well-stated research question. When this element is satisfactorily achieved, the broader research problem, the subsidiary questions, the terms, and even the analytical technique fall into place. As an adviser I am constantly amazed at the way in which the carefully drafted research question can focus the inquiry.

Some students (you may be one) prefer to develop together the first two elements of the proposal—the statement of the problem and the research question. They begin with a statement of the problem: "The purpose of this study is to discover the relationship between A and B." Next they state the research question: "If there is a change in A, will there also be a concomitant change in B?" Finally, they may offer a prediction, or hypothesis: "An increase in A will be accompanied by a concomitant increase in B."

Notice that they begin with an assertion of relationship; then they speak of that relationship in terms of a change in both A and B; and finally, they predict the direction that change will take. Obviously, I have grossly simplified what is often a very complex process; but the example highlights the close affinity between problem, research question, and prediction (or hypothesis). Some scholars insist that the problem and the question are one and the same, and they have a good point; but I claim it is not always so; in any event, when one drafts the formal proposal, it is useful to think of problem and question as separate, albeit closely related.

Earlier, we discussed the formulation of the research question in general terms. Now let us inspect an example from a sample proposal by doctoral candidate John Weygand. Notice that Weygand begins with an introduction and a statement of the problem, then casts his research and subsidiary questions, and finally defines his terms. Pay special attention to the way in which the four elements are linked. (An abbreviated version of Weygand's proposal appears as Resource A. Resource B is a proposal for an experimental study.)

The Carnegie Institution of Washington, 1901–1904:

Andrew Carnegie, Daniel C. Gilman, and John S. Billings

Search for the Exceptional Man

The Research Problem

On the eve of his retirement as the first president of the Johns Hopkins University, there came to Daniel Coit Gilman the opportunity to direct the fortunes of an institution that promised to become the most important research enterprise in the United States. Moreover, with the financial backing of the institution's founder, Andrew Carnegie, who had set aside as an endowment United States Steel bonds worth ten million dollars, Gilman faced the refreshing prospect of guiding an institution that was free of budgetary deficit.

But Carnegie and Gilman were not to be the only principals in this new adventure: John S. Billings, who was for many years a member of the United States Surgeon General's office and by 1901 the director and organizing genius behind the New York Public Library, was to serve the new enterprise as chairman of the Board of Trustees during its formative years.

It is a measure of the feverish activities of the institution that, by the end of 1904, five of the six research enterprises that continue to this day were begun: the Mount Wilson and Palomar Observatories; the Genetics Research Unit at Cold Spring Harbor, New York; the Department of Plant Biology at Stanford, California; the Geophysical Laboratory in Washington, D.C.; and the Department of Embryology in Baltimore, Maryland. Over the years the contributions of the Carnegie Institution of Washington have been varied and many. The institution has published hundreds of important research papers written by its own scientists and by scholars in other research agencies and universities. Contributions to practical affairs have been made, as well as scholarly findings designed to uncover the basic nature of the universe.

Improved ceramics, mining methods, hybrid corn, Pyrex glass,
and radar are just a few achievements to which the
institution has contributed in some way.

Clearly, then, any full understanding of the
development of American scholarship and science must include
a detailed knowledge of the growth and contributions of the
Carnegie Institution of Washington during its early years.
Moreover, any understanding of the early years of the
institution must be based on knowledge of the influence
exerted by the three most prominent contributors to the
activities initiated during those first years. On the basis
of my preliminary study, it appears that Carnegie, Gilman,
and Billings were the principal figures in charting the
destiny of the enterprise; however, other figures, such as
Charles D. Walcott, S. Weir Mitchell, Seth Low, Henry
Higginson, and Andrew D. White, contributed to the affairs
of the enterprise.

Besides providing information on the contributions of
the institution, the parts played by several major figures
in making those contributions possible, and the other
influences on the affairs of the institution, the present
study, it is hoped, will test Laurence Veysey's thesis on
the importance of purpose and control in an institution
whose mission is similar to that of a research university.

The Research Question

How were the fortunes of the Carnegie Institution of Washington influenced during its formative years, 1901–1904, by its chief financial benefactor, Andrew Carnegie; its first president, Daniel C. Gilman; and the chairman of its Board of Trustees, John S. Billings?

Subsidiary Questions

1. What position did each of three principals take with regard to the future of scholarship generally and of scientific scholarship in particular?

2. What view did each principal have of the future of the institution?

3. Precisely what part did each principal play in deciding the major questions to come before the Executive Committee? The Board of Trustees?

4. How did each principal think the C.I.W. should be controlled and directed?

5. What was it in the experience of each that contributed to his view of the best means for control and direction?

6. What were the personal and professional relationships between each of the three principals? Between the principals and others influential in the affairs of the institution?

7.   From whom did the principals receive advice?
Charles S. Peirce, Theodore Roosevelt, T. C. Chamberlin, J.
Franklin Jameson, Charles P. Steinmetz, Albert A. Michelson,
Alexander Agassiz, George Hale, and others.

8.   What part did other prominent figures play in
the institution's affairs? Men such as Andrew D. White,
Charles D. Walcott, S. Weir Mitchell, and Henry S.
Pritchett.

9.   By what process were decisions made?

10.   What models were available to guide decisions?
Did the principals know, for example, of the workings of the
Smithsonian, the National Academy of Sciences, the Nobel
Prize Committee, the Royal Society, and the like?

11.   How did the C.I.W. expend its funds? What
changes were made between 1901 and 1904 in the way funds
were disbursed?

12.   How satisfied were the principals (and others)
with the way the institution had developed?

13.   What relationship was there with the major
universities, especially those engaged in research?

14.   What was the response of the press and the
scholarly community to the institution?

Terms

Formative years: The years 1901 to 1904 are called the
"formative years" because in that period the institution

assumed tangible form and launched many of its important
projects and five of its permanent enterprises.

Fortunes: The word fortunes is used here to include
the achievements of the C.I.W., its successes and failures,
and the correspondence between those achievements and the
institution's major purposes and governing philosophy.

Influence: The "influence" of each major character on
the "fortunes" of the C.I.W. will be determined by the
extent to which each is able to convert his opinions and
attitude on questions of purpose, control, and major
undertakings into tangible achievement or policy.

John Weygand wanted to find out as much as possible
about the founding and early years of the Carnegie Institution of
Washington, but he realized that he would not have time to
explore all the fascinating persons, events, and achievements
associated with the institution. His preliminary reading and
thought, however, persuaded him that a properly stated research
question could take him to the heart of the matter. You see the
result in the question above. Notice, too, the subsidiary questions: (1) "What position did each of the three principals take
with regard to the future of scholarship generally and of scientific scholarship in particular?" (2) "What view did each principal have of the future of the institution?" And so on. Weygand
listed these and other questions as "subsidiary questions"—the
answers to which would shed light on the major research question and, if all went well, solve the research problem. At least,
that was Weygand's hope.

Let me give you a warning about subsidiary questions.
Some students seem to believe they should ask as many subsidiary questions as they can think of. Advisers sometimes refer to
this as the "shotgun" approach and usually discourage it. To

avoid this pitfall, I suggest that you test each subsidiary question with another question: "Will the answer to this subsidiary question really contribute something vital to the answer to my prime research question?"

Review of Relevant Research and Theory

With your research problem, research question, and subsidiary questions (and terms) well in hand, you are free to turn your attention to the next element of the formal proposal: the review of relevant research and theory, sometimes called the "review of the literature." In my experience, students achieve better results when they approach the "review of the literature" section of the proposal with an emphasis on the development of ideas; that is, when they treat "authors of important research . . . as secondary to the ideas they developed" (Stock, 1985, p. 43). Your task, as I see it, is to present a sample—a representative sample, if possible—of the *important* findings of relevant studies and theory, and not a mere list of everything ever written on the subject. Nevertheless, to select only the truly germane works, you may have to examine many studies with an eye both to the quality of their findings and to the limitations of their methods before you make a decision on whether to include them in your review.

You will recall that in Chapter One of this book I suggested that you create a personal computer database in which to record information on the important books, articles, monographs, dissertations, papers, theories, and interesting ideas you encounter in your study. This database should be more than a simple list of titles and ideas. For each item you should enter information such as author, title, date, subject, publisher, and summary of findings. In addition, enter your comments on the method of analysis employed, the quality of the findings or conclusions, major strengths and weaknesses, and any other pivotal information. If you follow this procedure from the very beginning, it will significantly enhance your ability to prepare the "review of the literature" section of both the proposal and the completed dissertation.

Before we turn to see what John Weygand did with this

portion of his proposal, I should like to call your attention to a feature of this element often overlooked by authors of dissertation proposals. It is overlooked, I suspect, because some subtlety is involved: subtlety that springs from the close relationship between problem, question, and relevant research and theory. To make this point clear, let us return to a previous example: the one in which a student might begin by asking the relationship between A and B, and then ask what change in A is accompanied by a change in B, and then predict that an increase in A would result in an increase in B. Whenever you predict that a change in A will be accompanied by a concomitant change in B, you should have a good reason for your prediction. Perhaps you have found some evidence to support the prediction; or you may have knowledge of findings by other scholars that lend direct support to the prediction; or you may have respect for a theory (or even have invented one) that supports the prediction. Ideally, of course, you might have direct support in both evidence and theory. In any event, if you have evidence or theory that directly supports your contentions, questions, or predictions, you should discuss that evidence or theory in your proposal.

In addition to discussing the theory or evidence that *directly supports* your questions, predictions, or contentions, you should review the important literature that *bears on* these questions, predictions, and contentions. It is not always easy to decide the difference between something that "directly supports" and something that merely "bears on." But the distinction is there. In any event, once you have decided precisely what directly supports your topic, what bears on it, and what is only interesting, you will be in a better position to keep the review of relevant research and theory section—the "review of the literature" section—under tight control. That is, you will avoid one of the common temptations most students encounter with their proposals: the temptation to submit page after page of prose devoted to the review of books, studies, reports, monographs, and the like, that often have only the most tangential relationship to the topic proposed for study.

The place of theory in scholarly research is a matter hotly debated in some circles (see the detailed discussion in the section on "Procedure," under the heading "Theoretical or Conceptual Framework"). Several disciplines work with highly developed theories, in the hope that the cumulative effects of scholarship will lead to better explanations, which may in time even be designated laws. Some disciplines use primitive theories, and there are scholars who insist that they use no theory at all. "I don't work that way" may be all one can coax from them.

In the example below, the author, John Weygand, worked with a theory — or perhaps some would call it a simple thesis. At any event, he permitted his inquiry to be guided by a thesis (or theory) advanced by another scholar, Laurence Veysey: In the development of American universities in the late nineteenth century, important academic conflicts arose over questions of basic purpose and the kind and degree of control that should be exercised by institutional leaders. Thus, when Weygand used the word *fortunes* in his research question, he defined that word in such a way as to include *purpose*, and he made *control* an important element in his subsidiary questions. Of course, Weygand might have chosen other theses or theoretical frameworks to guide his study, but he chose Veysey's thesis because it seemed to go straight to the heart of the matter. In any event, he did choose a thesis from a highly regarded piece of scholarship to frame his own approach.

Review of Relevant Research and Theory

The most impressive book dealing with the history of

the American university in its formative years between 1865

and 1910 is that of Laurence Veysey, The Emergence of the

American University. It is Veysey's contention that "the two

most important types of academic conflict in the late

nineteenth century were over the basic purpose of the new

university and over the kind and degree of control to be

exerted by the institution's leadership."[1] Whether or not
Veysey proves his thesis is, of course, a matter for debate;
that he marshals impressive evidence in support of his
conclusions seems certain.

The Carnegie Institution of Washington, to be sure,
was not a university; however, it did have part of the same
mission—research; if Veysey's thesis is correct, therefore,
one should expect to find in the C.I.W. the same conflict
found in the new universities. Moreover, because the affairs
of the enterprise were to be determined by Carnegie, Gilman,
Billings, and others—persons who had come from the worlds
of academe, business, science, medicine, and government—it
is reasonable to expect some fundamental differences of
opinion on questions of purpose and methods of control.

At this point a word of warning is in order. In work
of this kind, the aim is to find relationships from which
some general or special theory can be extended, qualified,
modified, corrected, or, perhaps, abandoned in favor of some
new theory. However, as Lawrence Stone and his colleagues
point out in Schooling and Society, it is extremely
difficult to find clear relationships.[2] Nevertheless, the

---

[1]Laurence Veysey, The Emergence of the American
University (Chicago: University of Chicago Press, 1965), p.
viii.

[2]Lawrence Stone, ed., Schooling and Society (Baltimore:
Johns Hopkins University Press, 1976), p. xi.

Veysey theses do provide an excellent point of departure,
and--who can say?--perhaps one day they will constitute a
fully developed and solid special theory on which to base
additional scholarship for this most important portion of
American intellectual history.

In addition to the pivotal work of Veysey, a number of
other primary and secondary sources are of special value to
this work. In 1970 an excellent biography of Andrew Carnegie
by Joseph Frazier Wall appeared to eclipse earlier
biographies such as John K. Winkler's Incredible Carnegie:
The Life of Andrew Carnegie and Burton J. Hendrick's The
Life of Andrew Carnegie. Of course, Carnegie's Autobiography
of Andrew Carnegie will be consulted along with other books
and articles about the benefactor. Emphasis will be placed
in these researches on primary sources, especially those
found in collections such as the Library of Congress with
its extensive holdings of Carnegie papers. There are
biographies of Gilman--one by Abraham Flexner entitled
Daniel Coit Gilman and one by Francisco Cordasco with the
same title. Useful, too, to these studies will be Hugh
Hawkins's Pioneer: A History of the Johns Hopkins
University, in which Gilman's activities are recounted and
analyzed. John Shaw Billings: A Memoir, by Fielding H.
Garrison, will be consulted along with a "Biographical
Memoir of John Shaw Billings" presented to the annual

meeting of the National Academy of Sciences in 1916 by S.
Weir Mitchell.

I will examine, of course, newspapers in New York,
Boston, Washington, Baltimore, Chicago, and elsewhere, as
well as a sample of scholarly and popular journals, among
them the American Journal of Sociology, Annals of the
American Academy of Political Science, Athenaeum, Century
Magazine, Chautauquan, Cosmopolitan, Dial, Education Review,
Engineering Magazine, Forum, Harper's Bazaar, McClure's,
Nation, New England Magazine, North American Review, Popular
Science Monthly, Quarterly Journal of Economics, Scientific
American, Scribner's, Science, American Engineer, and
others.

Although chief reliance will be placed on the primary
sources listed in the "Procedure" section of this proposal
and the literature already cited, I will study the
literature on the history of American higher education,
including John S. Brubacher and Willis Rudy, Higher
Education in Transition, and Frederick T. Rudolph, The
American College and University: A History, as well as the
literature on the history of science, including such works
as A. Hunter Dupree, Science in the Federal Government;
Howard S. Miller, Dollars for Research: Science and Its
Patrons in the Nineteenth Century; and Daniel Kevles, The
Physicists....

Procedure

Once you have set forth the research problem, worked out the research question and subsidiary questions to your satisfaction, and explored the research and theory that directly support and bear on your topic, you must set forth precise steps you propose to take to answer your question and solve your problem. Anyone who reads your proposal will want to know the theoretical or conceptual framework (if any) you intend to employ, the sources and quality of evidence and authority you will consult, the research design you will use, the analytical technique you will employ, and a timetable you will follow.

Earlier, I said that the procedure element is often the weakest part of the dissertation proposal. Moreover, there is scarcely a thesis adviser who has not heard one or all of the following rationalizations for dispensing altogether with a detailed set of procedures: "I can always get help with the procedural details later." "I don't want to be rigid. It's important to remain flexible." "Planning tends to inhibit the free play of intuition. I work best when I do what comes naturally." The systematic approach, contrary to what these rationalizations suggest, does not rule out serendipitous findings; indeed, it makes them more likely. However, the essential goal is always to provide an answer to the research question and problem.

What is needed is a clear and sufficient description of the procedures to be employed, the steps to be followed, so the reader will be persuaded that there is a direct line of thought leading from the statement of the problem to the activities of the scholar. The reader should be convinced that what is proposed is an intelligent approach to the problem and that, although no guarantees are given, there is a reasonable chance that an answer to the problem will be forthcoming.

Theoretical or Conceptual Framework. One of the first steps in developing a plan of attack for many scholars is to determine what theoretical or conceptual framework is most appropriate for the work at hand. This is an extremely challenging and controversial aspect of the entire dissertation venture, since

scholars often disagree on what constitutes a superior theoretical structure. Indeed, they are no more in agreement on the
role of theory in research than on the nature of research itself.

So important do some scholars consider theory that they
make a distinction between science and other realms of scholarship by defining science as those disciplines in which "elaborate theoretical structures have been developed" (Tullock, 1966,
p. 60). Kerlinger (1977, p. 5) has said that "the basic purpose of
scientific research is theory." He adds that a good theory, properly seen, "presents a systematic view of phenomena by specifying relations among variables, with the purpose of exploring
and predicting the phenomena." In psychology he recognizes
two levels of theory: on one level, the larger theories, such as
"Gestalt, behavioristic, psychoanalytical, and cognitive"; on the
other, more specific theories, such as those that attempt to deal
with intelligence, attribution, reinforcement, and the like (p. 10).

Berkhofer (1969, p. 6) states that theory is an integral part
of the behavioral approach to history but asserts that this discipline is one in which it is difficult to find agreed-upon models
for the solutions to problems. Consequently, each approach
must be a personal one to some extent and must be built anew
from definitions and ideas. And one of the most impressive
examples of "building anew" is found not in the work of a
historian but in the work of the nineteenth-century abbot and
botanist Gregor Mendel, who postulated unobservable agents to
account for inheritance characteristics in plants, agents ultimately identified only long after Mendel's death as based in the
genes and chromosomes of the cell (Thackrey, 1967, p. 80).

As you doubtless are aware, this is a complicated subject.
Volumes have been written on it, and many attempts have been
made to classify theories, often according to scope. There are
the grand or wide-ranging theories—Darwinism and Marxism
are two eponymous examples; middle-range theories, such as
behaviorism; and the even more limited theories designed to
explain specific instances or special cases. Some theories once
widely held—alchemy and phrenology, for example—have been
discredited. Others, while still accepted, are known only to
specialists. An example is "gauge theory," which I understand

has been posited for years in the field of high-energy physics. When I searched the *Comprehensive Dissertation Index* for the years 1983 to 1987 (the *Comprehensive Dissertation Index* is an index to *Dissertation Abstracts International* and several other sources on dissertations; cumulative indexes are available for the periods 1861–1972 and 1973–1977 and are updated annually), I discovered eighty-four doctoral dissertations in which "gauge theory" (or closely related topics) figured prominently. If "gauge theory" is of interest to so many doctoral students, can one assume that "gauge theory" is important to many physicists?

But the word *theory* is not easy to define. *Webster's New World Dictionary* (2nd College Edition, 1980), for example, has six definitions. One that seems to apply here is definition number 4: "a formulation of apparent relationships or underlying principles of certain observed phenomena which has been verified to some degree." But definition number 2 is also interesting: "A speculative idea or plan as to how something might be done." *Webster's* also informs the reader as follows: "Theory. . . implies considerable evidence in support of a formulated general principle explaining the operation of certain phenomena." I wonder whether "gauge theory" may be popular because it is backed by considerable evidence to explain "the operation of certain phenomena." According to Rivers, scholars "think first of building theory, but not *theory* as the term is used colloquially to describe a vague notion. Natural scientists and behavioral scientists consider theory a system of laws or a coherent body of general propositions that explain relationships and events. A body of theory enables a researcher to hypothesize, to offer possible explanations of certain relationships, then to test them to determine whether they should be added to, or substituted for, existing theory, which is always tentative" (1975, p. 6).

You will have many questions about these matters. How much evidence, for example, must one have before being confident enough to call an "explanation" a "theory"? What about all those "theories" for which there is little or conflicting evidence, or which are challenged by rival theories based on the same evidence? And how do you proceed in the absence of theories? Or suppose there is a theory that "explains" event *E*, but no theory that explains event *X*, even though the two events have certain similarities. Can one try to learn whether the predictions for event *E* made by theory *A* also apply to event *X*?

Does one have to be a philosopher specializing in epistemology to be a successful researcher? Surely a solid grounding in the nature of knowledge would be of value to someone seeking the Doctor of Philosophy degree; however, the task at hand is to find a theoretical framework within which to pursue a research problem. Although you should consult the research manuals in your specific discipline for an authoritative treatment of this important subject, the following authors are representative of those who have written on the general topic: Belth (1977), Benson (1972), Berkhofer (1969), Black (1962), Blalock (1985), Boulding (1970), Brodbeck (1959, 1968), Campbell (1988), Hesse (1966), Kaplan (1971), Parsons and others (1961), and Tullock (1966).

One way to arrive at an appropriate theoretical framework is to ask oneself some specific questions that will set the creative thought processes in motion. Examples: "Is there a theory, a variant of some theory, or a set of generalizations to which my research problem has reference?" "Would the Murray needs-press paradigm be useful for my purposes?" "Does Henry Adams's thesis on the exponential rate of scientific progress provide a framework for my own study?" "Does behaviorism afford the most profitable rationale on which to base my hypotheses?" "Do the views of Piaget seem to explain much of the variation I see in the data I have examined so far?" "Does Guilford's approach make the most sense in my circumstances?" "Could the tensions evident in the behavior of the subjects to be studied be accounted for by means of an adaptation of Festinger's cognitive dissonance thesis?"

If you have devised your own theory or model to explain an event, phenomenon, variable, or the like, this is the place to expound it. In his *Foundations of Behavioral Research*, Kerlinger (1986, p. 10) remarks that he does not "discredit or denigrate research that is not specifically and consciously theory-oriented." But he goes on to say, "Ultimately, most usable and satisfying relations. . . are those that are the most generalized, those that are tied to other relations in theory."

John Weygand's statement of conceptual framework is brief—partly because he linked his analytical technique to the conceptual framework in a somewhat unusual way:

The study I propose is based on a thesis by Laurence Veysey, who identified fundamental conflicts within American universities in the late nineteenth century. Predicated on this thesis is a major research question augmented by fourteen subsidiary questions suitably modified to fit the Carnegie Institution of Washington, an institution dedicated primarily to research. Three pivotal elements—institutional purpose, financial support, and control of decisions—have been chosen for special scrutiny. To understand the early history of the Carnegie Institution of Washington, one must assess the ability of three major figures to influence each pivotal element. The three major figures were the founder, Andrew Carnegie; Daniel C. Gilman, the first president of the C.I.W.; and John S. Billings, longtime chairman of the Board of Trustees.

Sources of Evidence and Authority. The second component of procedure calls for a list of the sources of evidence and authority on which you will rely. These may include:

1. *Tests, questionnaires, observations, and other devices.* Are these instruments reliable measures? Are they valid? Will permission to use them be required? Have you designed the instru-

ments to be used? If so, are copies of these instruments attached to the proposal? Will a pilot study be employed?

2. *Documents.* What condition are they in? Again, will permission to use them be needed? Is the sample appropriate? Is it large enough? Will the generalizations have both internal and external validity?

3. *Population from which the subjects are drawn.*

4. *Limitations of the study.*

5. *Ethical considerations.* If human subjects are involved, has permission to use them been sought and granted? The protection of human subjects is discussed later in this chapter. (See also American Psychological Association, 1982.)

Once again, this section of Weygand's proposal is brief because he dealt with some of the evidence in an earlier section of the proposal, and because of the nature of the research proposed. Presumably, Weygand had reason to believe that the manuscripts he wished to consult would be available to him when he reached the libraries where they were held.

As I pointed out above, there are two major sources for this study. The first, that of secondary materials, has already been discussed under the "Relevant Research and Theory" section of this proposal. The second source, and the one on which major emphasis will be placed, is that of documents found in certain archives as follows:

1. Andrew Carnegie papers at the Library of Congress
2. Daniel C. Gilman papers at the Johns Hopkins University Library
3. John S. Billings papers at the New York Public Library
4. Andrew D. White papers at Cornell University
5. Charles D. Walcott papers at the Smithsonian Institution
6. The Carnegie Institution of Washington collection of documents, personal papers, reports, and

transcripts of Trustee meetings and Executive
Committee meetings

Analytical Technique and Research Design. As your third procedural task, you must analyze the evidence, indicating your
research design, the special techniques to be used (content
analysis? internal criticism? path analysis? analysis of covari-
ance?), and the charts and tables to be employed.

A useful suggestion is to design some of the major charts
and tables before the process of data collection begins. One
professor asks his students to include in the dissertation proposal sample tables with imaginary numbers. He believes that
this exercise will enable them to visualize the kinds of data they
can expect to find and thereby will direct their thinking. In
addition, it will help computer programmers or other advisers
to understand what the student has in mind. The *Publication
Manual of the American Psychological Association* (American Psychological Association, 1983) is helpful on this score. Even better is
the thirteenth edition of *The Chicago Manual of Style* (1982).

Another suggestion closely related to the foregoing is to
construct cross-breaks or cross-partitions as an aid in choosing a
research design and an appropriate analytical technique. A
cross-break is a simple way to demonstrate the relationship
between two or more variables (see Figure 1).

Although John Weygand did not include a cross-break in
his proposal, Figure 2 indicates how his thinking about his
problem might have been represented.

(In the "Method of Analysis" section of his proposal, re-
produced as Resource A, Weygand discusses "situational analysis," a special technique he proposes to use.)

In the preparation of a research design, a pictorial representation often can be effective. As an example, someone who
plans to administer a "treatment" (T) to a group of "subjects" and
to measure (M) the results might develop a research diagram as
shown in Figure 3.

Thus, on September 1 Experimental group 1 is measured
for some characteristic—weight, perhaps—after which something is done to Experimental group 1 (a "treatment" is adminis-

Figure 1. Two Examples of Cross-Breaks to Demonstrate Relationships.

Question: Have Republican congressmen who represented an urban constituency tended to support transportation bills more than their urban Democratic colleagues have?

Political Party	*Supporters of Transportation Bills by Congressional District*	
	Urban	Rural
Republican Congressmen		
Democratic Congressmen		

Question: Is there a relationship between the student's need to achieve and the student's expectations for a college if professional and working class is controlled?

	Relationship Between Need to Achieve and Expectations for a College, Controlling Class			
	Professional Class		*Working Class*	
	High Need to Achieve	Low Need to Achieve	High Need to Achieve	Low Need to Achieve
High Expectations for a College				
Low Expectations for a College				

Figure 2. Pictorial Representation of Relationships in Carnegie Institution of Washington Dissertation.

	Ideas on Purpose	Ideas on Control	Ideas on Direction
Andrew Carnegie			
Daniel C. Gilman			
John S. Billings			
Others?			

Figure 3. Pictorial Representation of Experimental Procedure.

	Sept. 1	Oct. 1	Nov. 1	Dec. 1
Experimental group 1	M1 T1	M2 T2	M3 T3	M4
Experimental group 2		M1 T1	M2 T2	M3
Experimental group 3			M1 T1	M2
Experimental group 4			T1	M1
Control group 1	M1			
Control group 2				M1

tered). The treatment might be an experimental approach to learning, or a special diet, or an exercise program. On October 1 Experimental group 1 is measured again, and another treatment is administered, or a previous treatment is repeated or intensified. And so on until the last measurement on December 1. Experimental groups 2, 3, and 4 proceed according to a different schedule, and Control groups 1 and 2 are only measured and receive no treatment. Strict care is taken to ensure that the members of each group are as much alike as possible or that the method of analysis is chosen to adjust whatever differences are present. (For more suggestions on these matters, see Cox, 1958, 1981; Kerlinger, 1979; Winer, 1971.)

What formulas will be used? What computer programs? Since a simple change in the data collection process may make it possible to use a "canned" or "packaged" program, you might consult with a computer programmer early in your efforts — unless you are doing your own programming. If it is at all feasible, the "canned" program can be a great saving, provided no damage is done to the research design and no important data are lost. (See Hull and Nie, 1981; Klecka, Norusis, and Hull, 1982; Dixon, 1973, 1985.)

As already demonstrated, one good reason for pictorial representation of research findings — cross-breaks, tables, diagrams, and similar devices — is to make what you have in mind vividly apparent to others. Programmers, statisticians, or experts in documentary research techniques can give maximum assistance only when they know exactly what is planned. When the research design and analytical techniques are presented in a clear and understandable manner, a technical adviser is in a better position to suggest any needed improvements. In choosing a statistical technique, for example, you may have failed to take all the proper assumptions into consideration. At this point the programmer may offer valuable suggestions for simplifying the analytical procedure — assuming, of course, he knows precisely what is to be attempted.

Timetable for Completing the Dissertation. John Weygand's timetable was as follows:

Jan. 1–Apr. 1	Preliminary study: read biographies of Carnegie, Gilman, Billings, White, Mitchell, and others. Search for other references to C.I.W. Examine all published material available in university's library.

Apr. 1–June 7   Work in libraries as follows:

New York Public	5	days
Cornell	2	"
Johns Hopkins	8	"
Library of Congress	2	"
C.I.W.	30	"
Travel	6	"
Other	15	"

June 8–Aug. 31	Analyze evidence.
Sept. 1–Oct. 1	Write first draft.
Oct. 1–Nov. 1	Write second draft.
Nov. 1–Nov. 15	Polish and type.
Nov. 16	Give copy to adviser.
Dec. 15	Get copy back from adviser.
Dec. 15–Jan. 15	Rewrite and polish.
Jan. 15	Give new copy and abstract to committee members.

Feb. 15   Get comments back from committee
                          members.

Feb. 15–Mar. 15   Rewrite and polish.

Mar. 15   Give final copy to typist.

Apr. 15   Get final draft from typist.

May 15   Take oral examination.

May 25   Give final copies to committee members,
                          thesis secretary, library, microfilm,
                          and the like.

Trial Table of Contents

The trial table of contents provides a temporary organizational framework to give the reader some sense of the dimensions of the topic, and the researcher a temporary means for classifying note cards.

CHAPTER

    I.   INTRODUCTION

    II.   ANDREW CARNEGIE'S SEARCH FOR THE EXCEPTIONAL MAN

    III.   THE PROPOSAL DRAFTED BY DANIEL C. GILMAN AND

          JOHN S. BILLINGS

    IV.   THE BOARD OF TRUSTEES AND THE EXECUTIVE COMMITTEE

    V.   THE SUMMER OF 1902

    VI.   AN AVALANCHE OF ADVICE

    VII.   SOLID ACHIEVEMENT

    VIII.   GILMAN'S RESIGNATION AND THE REORGANIZATION

```
IX.   CONCLUSION

BIBLIOGRAPHY

APPENDIX
```

Brief Bibliography

A brief bibliography can help your committee members guide your reading and research. Furthermore, it will give them some idea of the quality and quantity of available source materials as well as your ability to find them. Your preliminary bibliography might include a few recent, pivotal journal articles, reports, government documents, and dissertations. Or you might provide a brief annotated bibliography in which you discuss the quality, quantity, and availability of significant databases or primary source materials such as letters, manuscripts, diaries, and autobiographies. Since a preliminary bibliography is usually the basis for the finished bibliography, work expended on it is never wasted effort.

Ethical Considerations and Use of Human Subjects

What moral principle should guide scholars in the conduct of their research? The answer: scrupulous honesty. The old biblical adage "He that is faithful in that which is least is faithful also in much" is one the scholar might well heed. Honesty demands, for example, that you abandon a pet theory when the evidence calls it into serious question; that you freely admit it when your study does not come out as anticipated; that you refrain from any manipulation of the data to obtain the results you had predicted. With so much riding on the outcome of your dissertation, you may be tempted at times to ignore data that seem at odds with a foregone conclusion, or to minimize them or shape them to suit your own purposes. But the temptation must be resisted if the dissertation is to remain uncompromised and the cause of scholarship advanced.

Still another ethical concern arises when the proposed research involves the use of human subjects who might be placed in situations of risk. The term *risk* goes beyond mere physical danger to cover any situation of stress, discomfort, embarrassment, invasion of privacy, or potential threat to reputation. This matter is a serious one in which the university will take a keen interest. It deserves careful thought on the part of the researcher.

What kinds of activities might involve risk? Certain experimental procedures, obviously; also, the completion of some kinds of personality inventories, questionnaires, or protocols. The use of certain films, recordings, documents, photographs, and tapes could conceivably entail some risk. So, too, might an activity that could involve coercion or produce embarrassment.

Again, the university will have prepared guidelines and established procedures to assist researchers in their dealings with human subjects (see also American Association of University Professors, 1981; American Psychological Association, 1982). In all likelihood, the department or college will have authorized a review committee to scrutinize such requests; the best course is to consult this committee before work begins. Since the committee members will want to know precisely what is planned, you should be prepared to answer such questions as these: Will there be any threat to the safety or well-being of the subjects? Any invasion of privacy? Will the subjects' identities be kept confidential? Will they be required to sign an "informed consent" form? If children or persons unable to give informed consent are involved, have extra precautions been taken for their protection? Will you explain all the possible risks and benefits involved? Will you inform your subjects of their right to withdraw from the activity when they wish?

The questions the human rights review committee will want answered may seem formidable, but they are essential to protect the rights of the subjects, the scholar, and society. It remains to be seen whether our laudable desire to protect the rights of human subjects will have the long-term effect of inhibiting scholarship and slowing the progress of human understanding (de Sola Pool, 1980).

Is the Proposal Binding?

Like many other students, you may wonder at some point whether it is permissible to depart from your proposal. You may, for example, come upon a different or superior method of analysis, which promises to serve you better than the one originally proposed. Assuredly, you may depart from your plan, but you must have good and convincing reasons for doing so. As a matter of course, any substantial divergence must first be cleared with your adviser, and possibly with the entire committee.

With any creative act—and the dissertation certainly qualifies as such—predictions are bound to be problematic, and proposals are a form of prediction. With this in mind, you will need to keep your advisers informed and seek their advice on any major departures from your proposal.

5

Employing Basic
Research Sources
and Techniques

Innumerable books have been published on conducting research in the scores of departments that make up the modern
university. As a conservative estimate, five thousand does not
seem an unreasonable figure; the actual number may be two or
even three times as large. To attempt to summarize in a single
chapter — even a single book — the diverse and specialized approaches to research represented by these volumes would be an
impossible as well as an impractical task. Therefore, for specific
information on how to conduct research in your discipline, you
will do well to consult one of the many books directed specifically to researchers in your field. This chapter will be devoted to
matters of general application: taking notes, avoiding plagiarism, understanding photocopying and copyright law, preparing tables and charts, and knowing when to quit.

Note Taking

In the section headed "A Recommendation: Learn to Use a
Computer" in Chapter One, I counseled familiarity with the
computer and advised you to begin a personal database in
which to record information gleaned from books, articles, lec-
tures, conversations, monographs, reports, papers, dissertations, and other materials. Because you may not own a truly

portable computer, you will probably find it necessary to jot down this information on cards or slips of paper and then transfer it to your database when you return to your computer. Some scholars take a lap-top computer with them to spare themselves the inconvenience of transferring these data. For my part, I suspect I will never shake the habit of carrying a few bibliography and note cards with me when I head for the library, lecture hall, and committee room. Although I know that there are distinct advantages to having bibliographical information on a computer database—for example, one can create bibliographies in any one of several different styles and can quickly retrieve information from note cards and rearrange it in countless ways—I still use the cards—out of habit, I suppose, and because I have found that they work for me. What follows, then, are suggestions on how to use bibliography and note cards. Fortunately, anyone who knows how to use the cards can profitably apply that knowledge to the use of a computer.

Two types of cards are recommended for taking notes: a *bibliography* card and a *content* (or note) card. Using a different color for each type will make it easy to distinguish between them and, if necessary, to separate them quickly and efficiently. Many note takers prefer the ample writing space afforded by the 5″ × 8″ card; others find the 3″ × 5″ card adequate.

The all-purpose bibliography card shown in Figure 4 is designed to allow a single card to serve for all types of entries: books, periodicals, newspapers, bulletins, surveys, manuscript folders, and so on. The reason behind the single card is to simplify the note-taking process and leave your mind free to concentrate on the substance of the works you are consulting. With the blanks on the bibliography card to jog your memory, you will automatically record all the essential details on a given source.

There is room on the card to enter the call number as well as the name of the library in which the book is located. The latter can be a vital piece of information, for in the process of preparing a long monograph, such as a dissertation or thesis, you may have to consult works in several libraries; should it become necessary to retrace your steps, you can easily do so. The "remarks" section on the bibliography card gives you the necessary space to record a brief critical judgment of the work in question. Such comments can form the basis of an annotated bibliography, which will have much to recommend it over a simple listing of titles. An even more thorough approach is to prepare an "essay bibliography," in which comments on each source are woven into a short, coherent essay (see sample in Resource C). One of the hallmarks of true scholarship, this form of the bibliography will be valued by the informed reader for its insights into the author's work and resources used.

There are many kinds of content (or note) cards. On one kind you may enter a quotation from a particular work; on another you may paraphrase some authority; on still another you may jot down comments or ideas that occur as you read, or make notes on transitions that will help your manuscript to flow easily from idea to idea, from paragraph to paragraph. These are but a few examples. Some authorities recommend labeling them as to type.

Figure 4. Bibliography Card.

CT 275 C3 W33
Call No.
Library: Suzzalo

1. Author Wall (Last Name) Joseph (First Name) Frazier (M.I.)
2. Title and Subtitle Andrew Carnegie
3. Publisher Oxford Univ. Press City N.Y. State
4. Periodical/Series
5. Class: Book ✓; Periodical/Reference ; Bulletin/Yearbook ; Report/Survey ; Newspaper ; Other
6. Year 70 7. Month 8. Date/Daily 9. Vol. 10. Pages/Columns 1137
11. Remarks Excellent biography; descriptions of A.C.'s complicated business dealings unusually skillful. Not much on Carnegie Institution of Washington. Does confirm what other sources say about A.C.'s personality and methods.

Figure 5. Content Card.

Carnegie
Topic

Page	Reference *Wall, A. Carnegie*
861	"*of all Carnegie's philanthropic trusts, Carnegie Institution of Washington received the least amount of criticism from the lay public and the academic world.*"

One of the most useful features of the content card, as illustrated in Figure 5, is the *slug*, or handwritten heading that appears above the word *Topic* at the top of the card. These headings serve the invaluable function of classifying each card in accordance with the trial table of contents drawn up for the original thesis proposal. When you begin the actual process of composing the dissertation narrative, the slugs will enable you to put your note cards in order and to rearrange them if you adopt a new outline. With the slugs as a guide, reorganization is simple; a new slug is entered on the card, and it is refiled in its proper slot. Should the cards become disarranged, you can easily determine where each belongs, as well as where it has been in the course of any manuscript revisions. The slug also serves as a brief reminder of the information contained on the card, and it may suggest appropriate chapter and section titles.

It is advisable to write on only one side of the content card, since material on the back can easily be overlooked. If more space is needed, a new card should be used. The entry on the "Reference" line may be abbreviated or shortened for the sake of convenience.

Like the bibliography card, the content card has the advantage of forcing you to enter all the essential information. The reminder provided by the "page" column, for example, can prevent one of the most common and annoying oversights in note taking—failure to record the appropriate page numbers.

Plagiarism

Surely no one needs to be reminded that words copied verbatim from another's work must be surrounded by quotation marks. Neglecting to give proper credit for quoted material is to invite punitive action on the part of its author or the author's publisher or lawyer. Careless note taking can be the cause of unintentional plagiarism. For instance, if you jot down a direct quotation and neglect to put quotation marks around it, you may later forget that these are another person's words and therefore may use them as your own. However innocently done, plagiarism is inexcusable; even when it is unintentional, it is still plagiarism. Equally reprehensible are the less obvious types of plagiarism, such as piecing together several sentences, or changing a few words in a paragraph, or paraphrasing without citation. Sometimes the subtleties of such distinctions may leave them open to scholarly debate. However, you will do well to avoid any practice that is even slightly questionable. At all times, therefore, you should attribute direct quotations to their source; acknowledge the ideas of others; avoid using the terms of others unless they are placed within quotation marks; acknowledge with proper citation your debt to any source; and, keeping the reader constantly in mind, include page numbers, footnotes, and other guides that will make it easy to trace material back to its original source.[1]

Is plagiarism common? Clearly, many academics have encountered examples of plagiarism and others have harbored suspicions. Newspapers occasionally carry stories of persons— sometimes very prominent ones—who have been guilty of plagiarism in one form or other. What causes it? Doubtless there are people who, for whatever reason, set out intentionally to deceive. Short of disclosure and punishment, it is unclear what the academic world can do to discourage such behavior.

For most people, however, inadvertent plagiarism is the greatest danger. Although some would claim it is the result of ignorance, I believe, as noted earlier, that in many cases carelessness in note taking and the sheer volume of information dealt with are more likely explanations. As Thomas Mallon wrote on this distasteful subject in *Stolen Words: Forays into the Origins and Ravages of Plagiarism* (1989): "To some extent the history of plagiarism is a history of notebooks" (p. 111). When quotation marks are omitted from a note card or a notebook entry, or the source of the quotation is not indicated, the quoted material can find its way into the dissertation without attribution. Plagiarism cases that make the newspapers usually involve massive attempts to deceive; a little carelessness, forgivable though it may seem, nonetheless should be cause for concern. Attention to the discipline of note taking will help prevent any misstep.

Photocopying and Copyright Law

The scholar's work was lightened considerably by the invention of dry photocopying, which has made possible quick, inexpensive, and high-quality copies of documents, articles, books, and other materials. Freed of some of the drudgery of transferring lengthy quotations and statistics from primary sources to note cards, the scholar can now concentrate on more rewarding activities.

Most students will need no urging to avail themselves of the various photocopying devices. In fact, many will err on the side of overuse. Sometimes a simple note on an article—not a copy of the entire text—is sufficient. Remember also that vital bibliographical data on the source of the material must be supplied along with any photocopied excerpts. Suppose, for example, you made a photocopy of a page from a professional journal and then put the copy aside for a few months. When you return to it, you may discover that you have a single page of prose with a page number in the upper right-hand corner—and that is all. You do not know the journal from which the prose came, the volume number or year of publication, the number of pages, or even the title of the article and the name of the author. You are in trouble.

The Copyright Revision Act of 1976 (Public Law 94-553), which took effect on January 1, 1978, is the first major revision of copyright law since 1909. Aimed at protecting "original works of authorship fixed in any tangible medium of expression," it encompasses literary works, dramatic works, musical compositions, graphics, films, sculpture, recordings, and the like. Under the terms of this law, copyright protection is extended fifty years beyond the author's lifetime.

There was a time, fortunately long ago, when all dissertations had to be published. Today a dissertation is considered "published" when it is placed on the library shelves or otherwise made available for public use. Many universities require each author to put a standard "copyright notice" on each copy of the dissertation, usually right before the title page. This notice must consist of at least three elements: the word *Copyright* (or the letter *c* with a circle around it), the year of publication, and the name of the person who owns the copyright. Some universities require a "quote slip" in which the author agrees to allow copying of the dissertation for scholarly purposes, in line with the "fair-use" doctrine of U.S. copyright law, and authorizes University Microfilms International in Ann Arbor, Michigan, to sell copies of the manuscript.

For most dissertations the copyright notice may be all that is necessary; however, if your dissertation contains something that might be the subject of legal action in future — a description of an invention, for example — it might be well to ask the advice of your graduate school, your university legal officer, or your own attorney on the need to obtain a "copyright registration" from the U.S. Copyright Office. A fee, a form, and two copies of the dissertation are required. In any event these are matters on which I am not in position to give more than general advice; for further assistance you should discuss specifics with knowledgeable university staff members. The *Chicago Manual of Style* is an excellent source of information on copyright matters.

Now to the other side of the coin: Can you use something in your dissertation that was never copyrighted or is so old that the copyright has expired? An old novel or autobiography, perhaps? Yes, but you must identify your source by providing complete bibliographical information (name of author, title of work, place and date of publication, name of publisher, pages from which quoted material was taken) in a footnote, an endnote, or a bibliography. Such scholarly acknowledgment repays your debt to the author and serves as a guide to any reader who may wish to inspect the original source. Failure to acknowledge one's sources constitutes plagiarism and is reprehensible.

What about material that is protected by copyright? Under the doctrine of fair use, the courts have usually permitted photocopying for such purposes as research, scholarship, teaching, criticism, or newspaper reporting. Photocopying done by the dissertation writer certainly falls under the first two categories, and therefore seems an appropriate instance of fair use. Many published books and periodicals carry statements on one of the front pages describing the limits of fair use. But how much can you use without doing damage to the concept of fair use? Again, the answer must be that, if you have any doubts, you should consult the officials in your library or graduate school or your school's legal counsel. In their useful thesis guide, Miller and Taylor (1987) report that most of the university style manuals they surveyed permit thesis writers to use "excerpts of up to 150 words, provided they do not constitute a major portion of the original work" (p. 46).

Should you obtain permission to quote copyrighted material in a thesis or dissertation? Most publishers prefer not to be bothered by doctoral students seeking such permission. If you are quoting within the fair-use doctrine, it is probably unnecessary. However, if your dissertation is later accepted for publication, you may have to obtain permission to quote certain materials. To do so, send the holder of the copyright—usually the publisher of the book or article—a simple form listing the work, the pages and lines you wish to copy or quote, and the title and publisher of the work in which the material will be published. The form also should include a place for the copyright holder's signature. You might also ask your own publisher for guidance on this point.

Obviously, these are complicated matters; the fair-use doctrine, for example, is subject to various interpretations. However, no one supposes that the purpose of copyright legislation is to paralyze scholarship; on the contrary, it is to protect authors against unauthorized use of that which they have created. Let me repeat my earlier advice: If any doubt should arise in your mind, refer to your university's style and policy manual and seek the counsel of persons on campus qualified to answer your questions. William S. Strong's *The Copyright Book: A Practical Guide* (1984) may also be of interest to you.

Tables and Charts

Some of the guides to theses and dissertations published by graduate schools give assistance in the preparation of tables, charts, graphs, and drawings. If yours does not, you will find the *Publication Manual of the American Psychological Association* (American Psychological Association, 1983) most helpful with the design of tables, figures, graphs, and illustrations. In addition, the thirteenth edition of *The Chicago Manual of Style* (1982) has an excellent chapter on tables. If you are using a computer, your computer program probably can arrange your data in a form suitable for the dissertation. However, the labeling of tables, charts, and the like, requires considerable thought if your reader is to grasp quickly the information you want your tables and charts to convey.

Knowing When to Quit

Surprising as it may seem, some students do not know when to discontinue research and embark on the writing of the dissertation. They continue to gather data, take notes, look up references, conduct interviews, or rearrange note cards. They concoct new tasks to complete or devise trivial leads to follow — any excuse will do to avoid writing. How easy it is to contrive "reasons" to prolong research, since a complex research project is by nature always a little unfinished. As the Council of Graduate Schools (1991, p. 22) points out, however, at some point students will have to put an end to their research: "Students are plagued by the temptation to read one more article, run one more regression, incorporate one more argument, do one more experiment. Sometimes this is necessary in order to produce an acceptable piece of scholarship, but at some point students and their faculty advisers must decide that the dissertation is finished. . . . Perfection is not possible, and students should not be excessively delayed, or paralyzed, by its pursuit. . . . The dissertation is, after all, supposed to be the beginning of a student's scholarly work, not its culmination."

Fortunately, a carefully crafted research proposal with a schedule of activities and the date on which each is to be completed provides an obvious safeguard against this pitfall. Nevertheless, you must vow to respect the schedule, completing research on the date promised and writing the first rough draft of the dissertation without allowing yourself to be diverted until the task is finished. Some students draft sections of the dissertation as soon as the research for that section is completed, so that research and writing go hand in hand.

Once again, however, the adviser has a crucial role to play in the development of the dissertation. It is appropriate, therefore, that this chapter closes where Chapter Two began: with an affirmation of the salient influence of the adviser.

6

Using the Library
and Locating
Essential Resources

Dissertation research will take some scholars into the field, some into the laboratory, and almost all into the library at one time or another to use computers, consult references, track down sources, and make notes on their reading. Consequently, they will need to know what information has been recorded, where it is stored, and how it can be retrieved.

To assist in the search, the university library offers a wide array of services and resources, including staff librarians; subject area specialists; computerized bibliographical retrieval services; the card catalogue; interlibrary loan services; archival material; guides to reference books, to style and form, and to dissertation preparation; periodicals (journals, magazines, newspapers, reports); abstracts of dissertations, reports, and articles; dictionaries and encyclopedias; manuscripts; facts, dates, statistics; biographical information; and lists of foundations and grants.

Computer-Based Reference Services

More than ever the emphasis in modern libraries is on the do-it-yourself approach. As a result, the library's computer terminal is a most important tool, and terms such as *database*, *online search*, and *CD-ROM drive* have become an integral part of the scholar's vocabulary. With hundreds of databases to consult, you can assemble a bibliography, often complete with abstracts, in short order with some confidence that the search has been wide ranging and that the list contains current titles. A few of the databases are Economic Abstracts International, Mathsci, Medline, Philosopher's Index, Art Literature International, Sociological Abstracts, Geobase, Inspec, Metadex, Biotechnology Abstracts, Sedbase, Microcomputer Index, Supertech, Historical Abstracts, Rilm Abstracts (Music), Environline, Zoological Record Online, and ERIC (Educational Resources Information Center). Many of these databases are commercial products located elsewhere and referred to as "online" because they are reached by telephone line; others are in CD-ROM (Compact Disk–Read Only Memory) form and can be studied at a microcomputer terminal hooked to a "CD-ROM drive" or reader. Most databases are available free of charge or at small cost. Some of them, however, can be quite expensive.

To tap these resources, you must identify the proper databases and CD-ROM disks to consult; your librarian can give you a list of those available. You also must select appropriate key words to conduct the computer search. If you have a topic in mind and can come up with a few key words, you might consult the *Library of Congress — Subject Headings* (1988) to compare your choices with words used by the professional librarians who classify subjects. However, one impressive characteristic of working with computer databases and CD-ROM disks is that you can refine your search by conducting "free text" searches using single words as well as phrases. If your word or words appear in the title or abstract of a source, the essential information on the source will appear on your computer screen. When a source looks promising, you press a button to instruct the computer's printer to print a "hard copy" of the information for future reference. If you run into trouble, your library should have a "computer search specialist" or someone on the staff to offer expert assistance.

Librarians

No one needs to be reminded that librarians are among the scholar's most important colleagues and allies. When you cannot locate the necessary information, you can avail yourself of the services of the reference librarian, who is a specialist in library research facilities. In addition, many libraries will have subject specialists or persons responsible for the several divisions within a library, such as science, business, education, or medicine. If something you need is not available in your university library, one of these specialists will know how to tap the resources of the eighty or so members of the Association of Research Libraries in the United States; the thousands of public libraries; the Library of Congress, with its 21,500,000 volumes; the great private libraries, such as the Newberry Library in Chicago and the Henry Huntington Library in California; the libraries of the government agencies; the state libraries; historical association collections; and the libraries of professional societies. You may be directed to a computer database called OCLC (Online Computer Library Center), where you will find information on the holdings of hundreds of other libraries nationwide. A few scholars have found it necessary to do a bit of traveling in pursuit of a topic if the material to be studied is housed in a special collection. If Abraham Lincoln were to figure prominently in your thesis, for example, you might wish to examine the noncirculating Lincoln collections at the University of Illinois and the University of Chicago. Nevertheless, through the services of the interlibrary loan office and microfilm, many valuable resources can be brought to campus for close study.

Librarians who conduct computer searches of the various databases for students and faculty constitute a third group worthy of special note. With the emphasis libraries have placed on self-service or do-it-yourself procedures, however, the need for computer searches has declined. Yet another extremely important group of librarians includes those in charge of special manuscript collections, such as rare books or regional history collections, which advanced scholars may want to consult in their pursuit of data for the dissertation. Frequently, a single librarian performs several functions. Besides regular duty as a subject specialist, for example, the librarian may spend time at the reference desk or help students and faculty conduct database searches.

Some universities have a large main library and several branch libraries with collections of interest to the faculty and students in a specific department. The librarians who manage these branch libraries are frequently known by students and faculty as "our librarians," and they can be especially helpful in identifying, locating, and obtaining key resources for the dissertation.

The Card Catalogue

At one time every student was familiar with the card catalogue, which lists on a 3″ × 5″ card essential facts about a given volume: call number, author's name, title, publisher, place and date of publication, and number of pages. Many books are cross-referenced under more than one heading, with cards filed under author; title; and subjects, usually selected from an established list such as the *Library of Congress—Subject Headings* list. Most libraries use either the Library of Congress classification system or the Dewey Decimal System, devised by Melvil Dewey. Under either type of classification, you can quickly master the call number consisting of letters and numbers pertaining to your subject and locate needed materials with a minimum of searching.

Books not found in the library's card catalogue often can be traced through a master list such as *The National Union Catalog*, the *British Museum Department of Printed Books*, or *Books in Print*. Again, however, many libraries now have such printed sources as *Books in Print* and *MLA Bibliography* on CD-ROM. In addition, as mentioned, OCLC (Online Computer Library Center) is a large database with information on books, periodicals, recordings, and other holdings at hundreds of libraries. Your library also may have a CD-ROM setup such as WLN (Western Library Network), which lists the holdings of libraries in your region of the country. When you have found the books or other sources you wish to borrow, your library's interlibrary loan office can be of assistance.

Libraries may one day abandon the card catalogue with its thousands of cards, hundreds of drawers, and dozens of cabinets. Some have already done so, and others have failed to keep the card catalogue up to date. Still, the old system has its uses and will continue to exist as long as scholars have need of it—that is, until computer breakdowns are a thing of the past and until there are enough computers to serve all those with a need to consult a library's vast holdings.

Dissertation Abstracts International

The *Dissertation Abstracts International* is a service of University Microfilms International in Ann Arbor, Michigan. Published monthly since 1954 (although a brief list has been available since 1938), this guide is divided into (1) Humanities and Social Sciences and (2) Sciences and Engineering. Included are abstracts by authors of dissertations accepted by over 550 universities in the United States, Canada, and a few other countries. The complete copy of a dissertation can be ordered in photocopy form, slightly reduced in size, or on microfiche or microfilm. There is a fairly stiff charge for this service, of course. A *Comprehensive Dissertation Index* to the *DAI* is available.

Guides to Reference Books and Periodicals

The library shelves will yield a number of guides to basic reference books and sources. One that reference librarians often turn to:

Sheehy, E. (ed.). *Guide to Reference Books*. (10th ed.) Chicago: American Library Association, 1986. A guide to major reference books of all kinds from all over the world.

Another useful guide:

Gates, J. K. *Guide to the Use of Libraries and Information Sources.* (6th ed.) New York: McGraw-Hill, 1989.

To keep abreast of current developments, you will also need to tap the vast pool of information fed by journals, reports, books, newspapers, and other periodicals. *Infotrac,* available in many libraries on CD-ROM disk readers, provides recent information from 1,000 popular magazines and journals and is updated monthly. *Magazine Index* is another source of information on popular periodicals available on microfilm. It, too, is updated frequently. The printed guides to such publications include:

Poole's Index to Periodical Literature: 1801–1881. (3rd ed. rev.) Boston: Houghton Mifflin, 1891. In two volumes. Five supplements covering 1882 to 1906. This is primarily a subject index. Long the best source for the nineteenth-century periodicals, it is beginning to be displaced by *Nineteenth Century Readers' Guide,* which is proceeding backward from 1900. See also M. V. Bell and J. C. Bacon, *"Poole's Index": Date and Volume Key.* . . Chicago: Association of College and Reference Libraries, 1957.

Readers' Guide to Periodical Literature. New York: Wilson, 1900–. Semimonthly with quarterly and annual cumulations; about 130 popular periodicals are indexed by author and subject. (Before 1929 it covered many education journals now listed in the *Education Index.*)

A newspaper index can be as perfunctory as a card file; in such a case, you must do a little digging to find the information you need. At times like these, you will be grateful for:

National Newspaper Index, available on CD-ROM, indexes recent articles from the *New York Times, Los Angeles Times, Washington Post, Wall Street Journal,* and *Christian Science Monitor* and is updated monthly.

Center for Research Libraries. If your university is one of the 180 that belong to the CRL, you will be able to tap substantial amounts of archival and other material for your research purposes, including many local newspapers (on microfilm), college catalogues, and foreign journals. The CRL also has a large collection of foreign dissertations.

Newsbank Electronic Index on CD-ROM indexes articles from many U.S. newspapers on many subjects and is available on microfiche.

Nexis is available online and indexes a variety of U.S. and international newspapers and other publications.

Printed newspaper sources include:

Index to the [London] Times. London: The Times, 1906–. Bimonthly.

New York Times Index. New York: New York Times Co., 1913–. If an event has been reported in the *New York Times*, you may be able to fix the date and then consult the local papers for more extensive news coverage. This index comes out biweekly and is cumulated every year; the classification scheme is broad and detailed.

Other guides to periodicals are listed below. Be sure to find out whether the guide you want is available online, on CD-ROM, or both.

Biological and Agricultural Index. New York: Wilson, 1964–.

Education Index. New York: Wilson, 1929–.

Educational Resources Information Center. Washington, D.C.: U.S. Government Printing Office, 1966–. The local library may be able to give you a copy of ERIC holdings available on microfiche. ERIC is frequently available online and on CD-ROM.

Humanities Index. New York: Wilson, 1974–.

Index to U.S. Government Periodicals. Chicago: Infordot International, 1972–. A quarterly, cumulated every year. One hundred or so government periodicals — such as the *Monthly Labor Review*, the *Federal Reserve Bulletin*, and *Family Economics Review* — are indexed, and a computer-printed guide is published. Also consult *USGPO Monthly Catalog* on CD-ROM for

bibliographical entries in U.S. Government Printing Office's *Monthly Catalog* of government publications.
Social Sciences Index. New York: Wilson, 1974–.

To locate a periodical the local library may not have, you can consult a database such as OCLC (Online Computer Library Center) or a regional database such as WLN (Western Library Network) or the various indexes to international periodicals and the *Union List of Serials in Libraries of the United States.*

Statistics and Facts

Statistics are found under a variety of headings in the reference collection. The *Library of Congress — Subject Headings* list will guide you to the headings you need, whether they are commercial, criminal, judicial, military, educational, governmental, local, state, national, or international. Especially useful are the various guides to statistical sources, such as *American Statistics Index* (Washington, D.C.: Congressional Information Service, 1973–); *Statistical Reference Index* (Washington, D.C.: Congressional Information Service, 1980–); *Index to International Statistics* (Washington, D.C.: Congressional Information Service, 1983–); and U.S. Bureau of the Census, *Statistical Abstract of the United States* (Washington, D.C.: U.S. Government Printing Office, 1878–).

Biographical Information

A plethora of biographical information is available, from the detailed biography of a single individual to books that record biographical data on thousands of persons. The best place to begin is with the *Biography and Genealogy Master Index* (Detroit: Gale Research, 1975–), which provides citations to biographical sketches in several hundred works of collective biography and related sources.

Foundations and Grants

Many researchers and doctoral students need financial support. It is always best to begin by exploring funding available within your own department and graduate school. Many departments, for example, have special funds set aside to assist students working on dissertations. The Andrew W. Mellon foundation has just awarded funds to nine American universities to improve their doctoral programs. Some of these funds are to be distributed on a competitive basis to students who are making good progress toward their degrees. For specific advice on grant sources outside your institution, consult:

The Grants Register, 1985–1987. (9th ed.) New York: St. Martin's Press, 1984.

Grants for Graduate Students. (A. Leskes, ed.) Princeton, N.J.: Peterson's Guides, 1986.

Bauer, D. G. *The "How To" Grants Manual: Successful Grant-Seeking Techniques for Obtaining Public and Private Grants.* New York: American Council on Education and Macmillan, 1984.

Directory of Research Grants. Phoenix: Oryx Press, 1975–.

The Foundation Directory. (11th ed.) New York: The Foundation Center, 1987. Lists foundations by name, location, purposes.

Manuscripts

Archives, manuscripts, and other "primary" source materials are usually housed and organized separately from the other library materials. The best approach to locating essential materials is through the curator of manuscripts. It also pays to become familiar with the guides to various state and local historical society collections, as well as:

Hamer, P. M. *A Guide to Archives and Manuscripts in the United States.* New Haven, Conn.: Yale University Press, 1961.

The National Union Catalog of Manuscript Collections. Washington, D.C.: Library of Congress, 1971 and supplements.

7

Organizing, Outlining, and Writing

Sooner or later your research will be completed: the last note card filled, the last subject interviewed, the results of laboratory procedures and questionnaires and computer searches analyzed and tabulated. Now the formidable mass of raw data you have painstakingly gathered must be organized according to the logical unifying principle outlined in your dissertation proposal; and your findings must be committed to paper in lucid, economical, and persuasive prose.

Like the research proposal, most dissertations conform to a fairly standard pattern, with certain common elements presented in a more or less predictable order. Typically, the dissertation will begin with an introduction that allows the author to accomplish these tasks: (1) explain the purpose and significance of the thesis; (2) outline the major research questions or hypotheses; (3) define the major terms to be employed; and (4) discuss the method of organization, the scope, and the limitations of the study.

Next comes the body of the text, in which the author describes relevant research and theory, analytical methods, and theoretical framework. This section also provides answers to research questions, presents additional findings or conclusions, and suggests possibilities for further research.

In addition to these major textual elements, the thesis

commonly includes a preface, a table of contents, a bibliography, lists of tables and figures, appendixes, an abstract, and other supplemental materials.

Unfortunately, understanding the basic structure of the dissertation does not guarantee that the writing process will get off to a smooth, effortless start. Just at the point of beginning the actual composition, for example, some students yield to the temptation to postpone the inevitable. A few more note cards, another go at analyzing the data, one more interview, another source requiring verification—any excuse will do. And even those who approach the task with alacrity occasionally become frustrated as they search in vain for the elusive opening lines that will rivet their readers' attention. Writer's block, like procrastination, can afflict anyone, but you are less likely to succumb if you have carefully organized your material and prepared an outline for the manuscript you are about to begin. With these tasks accomplished, you can approach with equanimity and dispatch the important business of composing the discourse.

Sorting the Note Cards

If you have not already put your "content" note cards in order, now is the time to do so, allowing the topic headings (slugs) to dictate their placement. These topics should correspond roughly to the headings in the trial table of contents you drew up for your research proposal. Some writers use the slugs as a guide to preparation of a new, more detailed, outline; some have been known to compose the first draft directly from these content cards.

If the heading on a given card no longer seems appropriate for its position within the body of the narrative, relabel it and file it in its proper place. You may have to relabel three or four times as outline and text are revised. Some of the content cards will fit neatly into the structure as planned; others will require a certain amount of adjustment or will suggest a need for further refinement of the working outline. Still others, which stubbornly refuse to find their proper niche, will obviously need to be extracted and filed away for future use.

After you have sorted the cards and laid them out in some fashion that renders them easily accessible, you can interpolate the accompanying illustrative materials — tables, figures, maps, computer printouts, photographs, and the like.

Often it takes a sense of the whole dissertation to show precisely where certain ideas and data belong. Like a jigsaw puzzle, the pattern begins to emerge. Areas where the evidence is sparse or lacking altogether will now be apparent. If you are lucky, you will already have in mind the data needed to fill the gaps; if not, you will have to search further. No attempt should be made to write the entire dissertation on note cards, of course, but transitional sentences or paragraphs can — and should — be composed and inserted in sequence, so that when you begin to write, the text will flow smoothly from one idea, topic, or segment to another.

Outlining the Narrative

Outlining the narrative is for many a vital preliminary step to the writing of the dissertation. Time spent at this stage is well invested, for it will help you gain a sense of the narrative as a whole. It can be especially useful when the organization of the thesis promises to differ markedly from the original structure envisioned in the thesis proposal. In any case, an outline helps to ensure a clear and logical presentation of the material. As you attempt to impose a logical unified structure on an amorphous mass of data, the relationships and relative significance of your major ideas will become clear, material irrelevant to your topic will be revealed, and the most effective manner of presenting ideas, evidence, and conclusions will emerge. When you begin to write, of course, you may find that your outline is inadequate or at least needs to be modified. No matter: you will already have made a good start.

You already possess a skeleton outline of the dissertation in the form of the trial table of contents submitted with the research proposal. If your research has not broadened your

subject well beyond its original scope or taken it in an unforeseen direction, the trial table of contents can serve as the basis
for a topic outline or, with a little fleshing out, a sentence outline.
The two forms are illustrated below.

Topic Outline

The Carnegie Institution of Washington, 1901–1904:

Andrew Carnegie, Daniel Gilman, and John Billings

Search for the Exceptional Man

   I. Introduction: Veysey's thesis on the development of
purpose and control in the developing American
university applied to a research agency, the C.I.W.

  II. Higher education institutions in nineteenth-century
America

     A. Liberal arts colleges

     B. The emerging university

     C. Other major research agencies

 III. Motives, aims, and expectations of the major
participants and other intellectuals and educators

     A. Andrew Carnegie, founder

     B. Daniel C. Gilman, first president

     C. John S. Billings, chairman of the Board of Trustees

     D. Charles D. Walcott, first secretary

     E. Other influential figures

  IV. Organizational activities

     A. Statement of purpose

     B. Early leadership

V. Public reception of new agency

    A. Reaction in the press

    B. Attempts to influence purpose and priorities

        1. Efforts of national university supporters

        2. Response of liberal arts colleges

        3. Demands of graduate research

        4. Encouragement from official sources

VI. Early struggles for control

    A. Emergence of Executive Committee as dominant force

    B. Billings's influence

    C. Gilman's ineffectual leadership

        1. Absence during critical formative period

        2. Contemplative approach to duties

VII. Accomplishments of first season (summer 1902)

    A. Communication with scholarly community

    B. Formation of advisory committees

    C. Groundwork for subagencies

    D. Initial grants

    E. Policy statement

VIII. Reorganization (1903)

    A. New charter

    B. Gilman's resignation

        1. Search for successor

        2. Redefinition of president's role

    C. Revision of bylaws

IX. Conclusion: Effect of leadership on Carnegie

Institution in its formative period

A. Wording of original bylaws

B. Weak leadership by Gilman

1. Age and personal factors

2. His conception of president's role

C. Strong leadership by members of Executive Committee

You will notice that Weygand's trial table of contents, although adhered to with relative faithfulness, has been considerably fleshed out. Some changes have been made to accommodate essential information not available to Weygand when he drafted his proposal.

Sentence Outline

I. Forces that shaped the Carnegie Institution of

Washington in its formative period illustrate Veysey's

theories on purpose, direction, and control in late-

nineteenth-century American universities.

A. From the outset, a strong Executive Committee was

able to exert leadership, relegating the president

to a secondary role.

B. A heavy scientific bias was apparent in the awarding

of early research grants and the founding of the

institution's subagencies.

II. In the late nineteenth century, the American

educational enterprise responded vigorously to the

intellectual community's demands for increased graduate education and research.

A. Liberal arts colleges felt that their integrity was threatened by demands of graduate instruction.

B. New universities modeled on the European institutions were actively seeking funds to expand advanced instruction and research.

C. Agencies such as the Smithsonian Institution enabled a few scholars to pursue research without the burden of undergraduate teaching.

III. American intellectuals and educators applauded Carnegie's proposed benefaction and sought to influence its character.

A. Carnegie first considered founding a new university but balked at creating a rival to existing institutions.

B. Daniel Gilman, retired first president of Johns Hopkins, felt that a new university could make a valuable contribution to the nation's intellectual life.

C. John S. Billings wanted support for original research and advanced instruction as well as for existing laboratories and institutions.

Which form of outline will work best for you? To some extent, it depends on your own work habits. If you have the time and patience to construct a sentence outline, it may ultimately prove more useful. On the other hand, the topic outline is briefer and quicker to prepare, and may be the only practical way to handle a lengthy discourse.

Since the major purpose of an outline is to help you achieve a logical progression of your ideas, it follows that the outline must conform to certain structural rules. Before you begin your outline, you must choose an organizing principle that will dictate the order in which you present your material. Weygand's historical study of the beginnings of the Carnegie Institution of Washington lends itself to the chronological approach; within this structure he relies on flashbacks to discuss motivation and give depth to his characterizations. A scientific or experimental study might follow a different organizational principle, perhaps one that emphasizes cause and effect and deals with them in that order or the reverse. Still another method of imposing an order on the narrative is to present the major points in ascending or descending order of their importance, familiarity, complexity, or other property. There are, no doubt, many other more complex ways to arrange a given body of information. It is probably wise to try a straightforward approach first, however, since an intricate organizational structure may have little but its novelty to recommend it.

Writing the Drafts

With these preliminary steps out of the way, you can be reasonably sure you have done all you can to encourage the unimpeded flow of fresh and original composition. It is assumed, of course, that you have armed yourself with the essential tools of the writer's trade: manuals of style and form, publication guidelines for your field of research, dictionaries, thesauruses, and various reference books.

Early in the dissertation process—before drafting the thesis proposal, before taking a single note—you were urged to acquire a copy of your graduate school's guidelines for thesis preparation. In this publication you will find such essential information as recommendations on style manuals and specifications to which the finished manuscript must conform—the weight and composition of the paper used, the width of margins, number of required copies, and so on.

From time to time, even the reasonably proficient writer needs to consult a recognized authority on prose style. The following works are particularly recommended: *The Complete Plain Words* (Gowers, 1962), *Form and Style: Theses, Reports, Term Papers* (Campbell and Ballou, 1990), *On Writing Well* (Zinsser, 1988) *The Elements of Style* (Strunk and White, 1979), *Line by Line* (Cook, 1985), and *On Writing, Editing, and Publishing* (Barzun, 1986).

In addition, you should have access to general reference works on style and form in manuscript preparation. Some of these volumes should be on your own bookshelves for constant reference; others can be consulted in the library. *The Chicago Manual of Style* (1982), published by the University of Chicago Press, is perhaps the most comprehensive style manual available in English. Other valuable manuals include the *Publication Manual of the American Psychological Association* (American Psychological Association, 1983), the *MLA Handbook for Writers of Research Papers, Theses, and Dissertations* (Modern Language Association of America, 1988), and *A Manual for Writers of Term Papers, Theses, and Dissertations* (Turabian, 1987).

Every student must possess at least one good standard dictionary, such as the *American Heritage Dictionary* or *Webster's*. Writers interested in etymology often rely on the *Oxford English Dictionary* (1989).

If your dissertation requires tables and figures, the *Publication Manual of the American Psychological Association* (1983) and *The Chicago Manual of Style* (1982) will prove useful.

The dissertation will probably be longer, infinitely broader in scope, and technically far more complex to present than any of the essays, term papers, or reports you may have written; but the rules of good expository prose apply here as they do to any piece of writing, scholarly or otherwise. Anyone nearing the end of graduate study may be presumed to have mastered the rudiments of good, serviceable prose; if you can illumine your manuscript with occasional flashes of brilliance

or elegance of phrasing, so much the better. This is no place,
however, for the precious, the pretentious, or the pedantic. Instead, you should strive at all times for a clear, graceful, forceful,
and economical prose style. If you cannot express your ideas in a
lucid manner, even your most profound insights may seem
hopelessly muddled; if your phrasing is awkward, your most
ingenious arguments may sound plodding and unpersuasive.

   This book is not designed to serve as a manual of form
and style. Acknowledged experts in this field have already been
cited, and it is to these authorities you should turn for inspira-
tion and for clarification on matters of syntax and word usage.
Nevertheless, a few remarks on basic writing style would not be
amiss at this point. It is a rare piece of writing that cannot be
improved by careful attention to the details of word choice and
syntax. Compare the following wordy and rough first draft with
the improved draft that follows it.

(wordy—needs   The initial recorded instance of Dr.
to be
tightened)   Benjamin Rush's interest in a federal university

                is to be found in a letter which he wrote to his

                friend Richard Price on May 25, 1786. There was

                need, he said, for a "federal university under

                the patronage of Congress" in which "the law of

                nature and nations, the common law of our

                country, the different systems of government,

                history, and everything else connected with the

                advancement of republican knowledge and

                principles"[1] were to be taught.

                Rush went abroad to receive his own

(vague   medical training at the University of Edinburgh,
reference)
                causing his lifelong resentment of the lack of

                educational opportunity in his own country.

After returning to the colonies, Rush was a

(awkward—
lack of paral-
lelism in
compound
predicate)
(misplaced
modifier)

signer of the Declaration of Independence and

served as a member of the Continental Congress

and as surgeon-general of the Middle Department

during the Revolution, a position he resigned

after a disagreement with his superior. When the

(lack of paral-
lelism in com-
pound
predicate
again)

war ended, Rush was among the founders of

Dickinson College and published essays on the

reform of the prison system, abolishing slavery,

(sentence ele-
ments not
parallel)

and how to educate the young for life under a

republican system of government as well as a

variety of other subjects.

A grammatically tidier version shows much of the under-brush cleared away:

Dr. Benjamin Rush first recorded his interest in a

federal university system in a letter to a friend on May 25,

1786. What was needed, he wrote Richard Price, was a

"federal university under the patronage of Congress" with a

course of study that would include "the law of nature and

nations, the common law of our country, the different

systems of government, history, and everything else

connected with the advancement of republican knowledge and

principles."[1]

Rush had received his medical training at the

University of Edinburgh and, after his return to the
colonies, had had a distinguished career in medicine,
politics, and the military. A signer of the Declaration of
Independence, he also served as a member of the Continental
Congress. During the Revolution he was for a time surgeon-
general for the Middle Department, a position he resigned
after a disagreement with his superior. In later years Rush
helped to found Dickinson College and published essays on
social concerns of the day, among them prison reform, the
abolition of slavery, and the education of the young for
life in a republic.

As you begin your first draft, you may find that stopping
to hunt for the exact word or phrase only delays the process of
getting your essential ideas down on paper. That task is better
left for a later draft of the dissertation. On the other hand, this is
the time to insert your footnotes, placing them in the body of the
text rather than at the bottom of each page or at the end of a
chapter. If it becomes necessary to cut and paste later, the
footnotes will be close to their references, and there will be less
danger of losing a footnote or citing it incorrectly.

If you were conscientious about following your institution's guide to style and form, you should have no difficulty
providing all the information needed for complete footnotes.
Regrettably, some students have been known to complete a large
portion of their note taking before they bother to acquire an
authoritative guide; as a result, they find they have neglected to
obtain some information essential to proper citation or bibliographical integrity. (Examples of style and form manuals were
cited earlier.)

Instead of footnotes at the bottom of the page, some
authorities prefer footnotes grouped at the end of each chapter,

or occasionally at the conclusion of the main text. When placed this way, these "footnotes" are called "endnotes." Whether you employ footnotes or endnotes, be sure to give the page number in the reference cited, so that your readers can go directly to the source. For a somewhat different method of citation, common to journals in psychology, sociology, and other social sciences, see the "Sample Proposal: Experimental Approach" at the back of this book (Resource B).

Despite all efforts to flesh out the materials in the content cards before beginning the first draft, you may discover certain weaknesses in the narrative as the writing proceeds. More examples will be needed; certain segments will have to be shifted to other parts of the manuscript; topics that seemed essential to the text now appear to contribute nothing at all; charts presented in the body of the document may now seem to belong in an appendix. Modifications and improvements of this nature are important, but you will be better advised to grapple with them later. Instead, it is important now to press on to completion of the first draft. When you can view the work in its entirety, you can more easily form a critical judgment of what is needed.

As soon as the first draft is finished, have at least one photocopy made and stored where it will be safe from fire, flood, or other disaster; and do not forget to back up your computer disks. In the unlikely event of the destruction of the original, you will be protected. Working from a first draft, you may be able to salvage the entire dissertation, even if content cards, memoranda, computer printout, and other essential data are lost.

In the second draft, you can make any necessary shifts, additions, or deletions in the text. Do not hesitate to remove a passage from the body of the thesis and relegate it to a footnote if it interrupts the flow of the narrative or fails to contribute significantly to the whole. Later you may even decide that some of these footnotes are of no value and can be safely removed.

As you polish this second draft, try to provide the transitions that will lead your reader from one idea or paragraph or sentence to the next. Again, it is inadvisable to spend too much time deliberating over the appropriate word or phrase. The third, and in many cases the final, version will offer ample opportunity for making refinements in the text.

Early in the writing process, determine at what point your faculty adviser and other members of your dissertation committee should be shown the manuscript. The adviser may wish to read one of the early drafts, perhaps the second, or may prefer to see each chapter as it emerges from the typewriter. Before deciding when the entire committee should see copy, the adviser will want to make sure that the work has progressed enough to be evaluated in a constructive manner. If the committee members see the manuscript too early, the resulting comments and criticisms may be contradictory, confusing the writer and leaving in the minds of the members unfair impressions that will be difficult to dispel.

When the manuscript is finally ready, you should submit it to the committee in its entirety. Sometimes students fail to present such items as the abstract, the table of contents, the preface, or the end matter (bibliography, appendixes), on the assumption that the committee is interested only in the body of the text. Not so! Advisory committee members are responsible for the whole dissertation — not merely its content but also its form and physical appearance. Committee members who take their charge seriously will want to inspect the finished product before the final oral examination.

Preparing the Abstract

When the dissertation is finished, one extremely important writing task remains — an abstract of approximately 350 words (about a page and a half). This summary of your manuscript will appear in *Dissertation Abstracts International*. It is to your abstract that most scholars first turn to gain an understanding of what you have achieved. Some will decide to order a copy of the entire dissertation solely on the basis of the quality of the abstract.

Your task, then, is to prepare a concise statement that will tell your reader what the research question is, why it is important, what theoretical framework was employed in the research, what data were collected, how they were analyzed, what special techniques (if any) were used, and what results were found.

Some universities ask each candidate to prepare a longer abstract—six pages or more—to be distributed to each member of the examining committee just before the final defense of the thesis. However, unless the university gives instructions to the contrary, the 350-word abstract will suffice for both the defense and an entry in *Dissertation Abstracts International*.

A portion of John Weygand's abstract is given below:

Abstract

Within two years of its founding on January 22, 1902, the Carnegie Institution of Washington was well on its way to becoming one of the most important research enterprises of its kind in the world. The research question asked in this dissertation was "How were the fortunes of the Carnegie Institution of Washington influenced during its formative years, 1901–1904, by its chief financial benefactor, Andrew Carnegie; its first president, Daniel C. Gilman; and the chairman of its Board of Trustees, John S. Billings?"

Guided by a thesis put forth by Laurence C. Veysey, I examined major conflicts over purpose and control and employed a technique called "situational analysis" to answer the major research question and the fourteen subsidiary questions. Whenever possible, I used primary sources, including the papers of Carnegie, Billings, Gilman, Andrew D. White, Charles Walcott, and others....

Preparing the Final Draft

To prepare the final draft of their dissertations, many students use a personal computer equipped with the latest version of a popular word-processing program, including a spelling checker, a grammar checker, and a thesaurus. (Some of the more expensive software will prepare indexes and much more.) They type to a hard disk and back up everything on diskettes before printing the dissertation on a letter-quality printer or laser printer. They prepare extra copies with a laser printer, a letter-quality printer, or a photocopier. Computer software devised with one or more of the recognized style manuals in mind is coming on the market. Some writers—especially those in the sciences, technical fields, and mathematics, who must use special symbols—employ sophisticated formatting programs that are designed to produce superior copy on a variety of printers.

In the days before the advent of computer technology, candidates were routinely advised against attempting the final typescript of the dissertation. Every reputable graduate school and department will accept only near-perfect copy for binding and inclusion in the university's collection. Degree candidates, it was felt, were under enough stress in their academic careers without the added frustration of turning out an acceptable typescript. Moreover, students were discouraged from entrusting the job to a spouse or secretary unless they possessed the requisite skills and, in addition, were experienced in dealing with the intricacies of the scholarly manuscript. The specialized, sometimes esoteric, nature of the text, which might contain technical terms, formulas, or foreign words and phrases; the spacing and arrangement of footnotes, tabular material, charts—all these aspects of dissertation typing made the task a demanding one that was best handled by a professional.

Today the proliferation of word processors and computers has altered the situation significantly. Armed with the software and hardware now available, you may be entirely adequate to the task of producing an acceptable final manuscript, no matter how rudimentary your typing skills. If you lack the time, inclination, or the necessary equipment, however, you may want to secure the services of an experienced typist or word processor. Locating such a professional in the environs of a university is usually not difficult, but finding one who can meet the rigid standards of thesis manuscript preparation may be more of a problem. Fortunately, the office of graduate studies can be most helpful on this score. Indeed, one of the marks of a first-rate institution is the cheerful assistance it is willing to give scholars intent on producing excellent dissertations. One such service is the maintenance of an up-to-date list of qualified and experienced word processors or typists. Credentials of operators recommended by other sources should be double-checked with the graduate school office. Many institutions also staff a dissertation office with a secretary who inspects approved drafts to be sure they conform to standards of legibility and accuracy in footnoting, spelling, bibliographical form, and so on. The office can often then direct you to a competent person trained in thesis form and style.

Having taken pains to secure the services of an experienced typist, however, you cannot turn in poor copy and expect a miracle. In order to do a creditable job, even the ablest typist must have copy that is clear and understandable. It should be typed and proofread carefully; footnotes should conform to the formal style chosen; all information should be complete. Tables and charts must be shown exactly as they are to appear in the final copy; the bibliography should be free of error. Strikeovers or interlineations must be neatly done, so as not to confuse the typist. In short, the copy should be as free of error as is humanly possible. When you make an effort to provide good, clear copy, you will in the long run save time (yours and the typist's) and money, and both you and your typist will be satisfied with the results.

The mechanics of manuscript preparation will depend on your institution's requirements. Again, you will want to consult the office of graduate studies on such matters as the width of margins, weight of paper, type of ribbon, and appropriate typeface. Moreover, you should be given some idea of the costs involved: the rate per page, the cost of supplies, the cost of photocopying, and so forth. You will also want to know how many copies the university requires for binding; in addition, you may wish to have extra copies bound to present to the members of your dissertation committee.

8

Defending
the Thesis

The modern seminar room where thesis examinations often take place is vastly different from the forbidding interior of the hall in North Hungary described by Donald Davinson: "It is a vast and somberly magnificent place with a small gallery high up at each end perhaps two hundred feet apart. In one sat the candidate and in the other his opponents. The disputation took place over the heads of the assembly. The tension upon the candidate must have been very great" (1977, p. 19). The proceedings also are far more relaxed and informal than in the days when the oral defense of the thesis pitted candidate and examiners in a sort of verbal combat. As Davinson suggests, the candidate in such a setting was under enormous stress as he stated his thesis or undertook to defend one put to him, and then attempted to refute the challenges of the examiners.

Much the same pattern of questioning prevails today, although the candidate's stance is less likely to resemble that of a lawyer defending a client in court with every legitimate means at his disposal. Rather, he will often cite possible counterarguments and deal with them in the dissertation itself, as though in expectation of the committee's challenges. He will make an honest assessment of the strengths and weaknesses of his study, note any possible sources of error, and indicate when his comments go beyond the evidence he has gathered. Since accuracy is his primary aim, he will, in the words of Cole and Bigelow (1946, pp. 20–21), "expose the weaknesses of his position with the same care that he devotes to demonstrating its strengths."

Not all universities require an oral examination upon completion of the dissertation. Some critics of the oral examination insist that it has become a mere formality and that, if anything beyond approval of the thesis is required, the candidate should give a public lecture. "What purpose," the critics ask, "is served by an examination after a three-man reading committee has judged the dissertation acceptable? How could any committee, which includes the three readers, fail a candidate after a majority had approved the dissertation?" The fact is, of course, that some students do fail oral examinations despite approval of the dissertation by a reading committee: new evidence is brought out at the examination, opinions change, some students have difficulty expressing ideas under the pressures of an oral examination. Still, the critics of the oral examination advance an interesting point. To overcome objection to this claim, some universities do not insist that reading committees accept or reject the dissertation prior to the oral examination. Instead, the reading committee is charged to decide whether or not the dissertation is of sufficient substance to justify an oral examination, and to withhold final judgment until after the examination. A quibble? Probably not, but the difference between outright approval of the manuscript and "approval sufficient to justify an examination" may be a distinction easily blurred in the minds of some readers.

Institutions that require a defense usually set a minimum waiting period between submission of the manuscript and the oral defense. This interval gives the committee ample time to read and absorb the dissertation. Meanwhile, you should take the opportunity to review your study, so that you will be able to respond readily and authoritatively to questions on your goals, methods, and conclusions.

As you enter the examining room, there are two encouraging thoughts for you to bear in mind: (1) you know more about your dissertation than anyone else; (2) everyone present wants you to succeed.

A little elaboration may be needed to convince you of the truth of these observations. If you reflect a bit, however, you will realize that your academic preparation and your months, perhaps years, of intense reading and research have given you a specialized knowledge of the topic that few others possess. You have had opportunities to consult with the individuals on your committee; you know how they would assess both the dissertation's strengths and its shortcomings. If you heeded their advice, you addressed their misgivings in the document itself. If questioned on any of these matters in the course of the examination, you can only review your written comments. Of course, when a question is asked to which you have no answer, you should be quick to say so. Chances are, however, that you will be able to respond to all the committee's questions.

Nor should you doubt that everyone involved in the oral examination truly wants you to succeed. This fact should illuminate the proceedings even when the questioning becomes a bit spirited. The better the dissertation, the deeper the committee may probe. They may even challenge you a bit to see whether you have the courage to support your conclusions. On your part, you should not hesitate to reveal your own enthusiasm for the project. After all, you have expended enormous amounts of time, energy, and money in producing the dissertation. Its successful reception will have important implications for your career. It is a good, solid piece of work, and you should be happy for the opportunity to discuss it publicly.

There is no doubt that a sound thesis ably defended is one of the high points of the academic experience. The glow of satisfaction the committee members feel when a student performs creditably can stay with them for days. Their vicarious pride and pleasure in her achievement are thoroughly understandable. After all, they have helped to guide and nurture her in the course of her academic career. She has attended their classes and sought their advice. Although the accomplishment is the candidate's own, her professors are bound to feel they have contributed in no small degree to her success. This is especially true of the thesis adviser, whose commitment of time and energy and whose stake in the project are second only to the candidate's. Inevitably, the student's performance reflects on the professional competence of her adviser in ways both subtle and direct.

In normal circumstances the defense of the thesis is conducted in a fairly informal setting, often a seminar room. Present are the candidate and the members of the examining committee, usually all of them holders of the Ph.D. degree and the rank of assistant professor or higher. (Some graduate deans are permitted to make exceptions to this rule, however.) Some universities may appoint a representative from another institution; in fact, a few insist on outside representation. Occasionally, graduate students will attend because of their interest in the dissertation topic; and nothing prevents the candidate from inviting friends. Still, the audience is unlikely to be anywhere near the size of those which in centuries past sometimes numbered in the hundreds and required the use of a large hall. In those days, too, it was customary for the candidate who had successfully defended his thesis to throw a party for all his friends and acquaintances. Accounts of these festivities reveal sometimes staggering outlays for food, drink, and entertainment.

Today practice at various institutions may vary, but in general, when the time comes for you to defend your thesis, you can expect the examination to proceed according to a similar pattern. When all the participants are present, the chairman may begin the proceedings by asking you to step out of the room while the ground rules are discussed. A few institutions have rules governing the conduct of the examination, even to the point of specifying the amount of time allotted for each departmental representative to question the candidate.

When you return and the procedure is explained to you, the examination begins in earnest. The chairman is usually granted the courtesy of asking the first question. This practice has the advantage of giving you a chance to relax a bit and gradually warm to your subject. Presumably, you will feel most at ease with the chairman (if the chairman is also your adviser), and your close working relationship will make any unforeseen challenges unlikely. At the same time, the other members of the committee will take their cue from the chairman, whose demeanor sets the tone for the rest of the proceedings.

As the examination continues, you should be prepared to answer a variety of questions, both general and specific. The early ones are often designed to reduce any feelings of anxiety and to draw you out. You might be asked to summarize the dissertation in a few sentences. If you have been at pains to produce an exemplary abstract, this task should pose no problem. Anticipating such a question, many students have in mind a twelve- to fifteen-minute summary they can call upon if necessary.

In a similar vein, you might be asked to discuss your major findings. Again, the intent is not to challenge you but, rather, to let you appear to your best advantage. Other questions in this category deal with your plans for further research; ideas for publication of the thesis, either in whole or in part; and implications of the study for the work of another scholar or group of scholars.

The examiners may also ask you how the dissertation qualifies as an original contribution to knowledge, what its major weaknesses are, and why a particular method of analysis was chosen. You may even be asked to suggest a research question to be used by someone interested in carrying the study beyond the limits of your own investigations. Sometimes examiners will ask such questions as "Are there scholars who might disagree with your conclusions?" "In what ways has this work on the dissertation contributed to your growth as a scholar?" "Were you to start afresh, would you do anything differently?" "Are there courses you think ought to be added to our curriculum that would have been useful to you in preparation of your manuscript?"

Sometimes a question will require a response that goes beyond the data or findings of the study. There is no harm in expressing an opinion if you are asked to do so; however, it should be clearly labeled as such.

If you wish, you may bring a copy of the dissertation to the defense; no doubt the committee members will have their copies with them. Minor editorial changes or other small adjustments in the text may be suggested during the course of the examination. Before any alterations are made at this stage, however, you and the members of your committee must agree that they are appropriate and necessary. Your thesis adviser (as committee chairman) is responsible for assessing the group will in these matters.

As a rule, it is unwise to burden the examiners with too much in the way of explanatory data. Nevertheless, students occasionally come armed with special charts, tables, and similar visual aids; some have even used an overhead projector to advantage in presenting key charts, statistics, or illustrations. Sometimes the blackboard is all that is needed.

When each member of the committee has had a turn, the chairman will call for further questions. If there are no further questions, you will be dismissed to wait outside or in the adviser's office while the committee members deliberate and finally put your performance to a vote. The Council of Graduate Schools (1990a, p. 27) reports that "almost all universities require more than a simple majority to pass the candidate. Some specify that a single negative vote fails the candidate, some that two or more negative votes are required to fail." In the event of failure, a waiting period (often three to six months) is required before the examination can be repeated. As a rule, only one reexamination is permitted.

As you await the committee's verdict, you will probably experience the familiar pangs of postexamination brooding. The brilliant analysis, the dazzling riposte, the precise word or term that eluded you as you defended the thesis now occur to you in abundance. Misgivings about the quality of your performance assail you, especially if the minutes drag on and you are not summoned back to the examination room. All these anxieties are natural and predictable. You must try to relax and expect a favorable outcome.

The process of evaluation should not be a mere formality, however. Each member of the committee will wish to make a comment or two; sometimes the more impressive the disserta-

tion and the candidate's general performance, the more pro-
longed the discussion. This may also be the case when things
have not gone well, of course. Nonetheless, you should not
become alarmed if some time elapses before your adviser calls
you back for the committee's decision.

Time will dull the memory of any uneasiness you may
experience while you await the committee's decision. What you
will never forget is the overwhelming sense of achievement that
is yours as you accept the congratulations of your mentors and
realize that you have now been admitted to the fellowship of
scholars, the company of educated men and women.

9

Adapting the Thesis
for Publication
and Presentation

Everyone who has ever written a dissertation hopes that it will serve as a useful resource for other scholars in years to come. Gratifying as it is to see one's work cited occasionally in a footnote or bibliography, many authors would be delighted to see their dissertations reach a wider audience. Must those neatly typed, handsomely bound manuscripts be left to gather dust on library shelves? Or is there life for the dissertation after defense?

In some cases, yes. Each year a few notable examples undergo a metamorphosis and emerge as full-fledged books, often under the imprint of a university or scholarly press. The dissertation of A. Hunter Dupree, a highly regarded historian of science, was enlarged and published in 1959 as *Asa Gray: 1810–1888*; in 1988 it was reissued in paperback form as *Asa Gray: American Botanist, Friend of Darwin*. The dissertation of David Gardner, president of the University of California, became *The California Oath Controversy* (1967); and Thomas M. Doerflinger's book *A Vigorous Spirit of Enterprise: Merchants and Economic Development in Revolutionary Philadelphia* (1986), winner of the Bancroft Prize for American history, began as research for an undergraduate thesis at Princeton. Doubtless one could cite other examples of dissertations that emerged as books, but most survive in modified or abbreviated form as journal articles or papers presented to the author's colleagues at meetings of the various academic or professional associations.

If your adviser and members of your supervisory committee recommend that you seek a publisher for your dissertation, should you follow their advice? Of course, but be aware of a danger. A recommendation to seek publication, while sincere and flattering, has impelled too many students to mail the raw dissertation to a book publisher, when, in fact, an article or a series of articles submitted to a professional journal is the more appropriate response. Unsolicited dissertations usually encounter little enthusiasm when they arrive in a publishing house.

In the early twentieth century, publication of the thesis was not the exception but the rule. The doctoral candidate was required to publish or have a contract to publish in hand before the degree was granted. Later, most academic departments dropped this stipulation, insisting only that an article based on the thesis appear in a professional journal. Mercifully, such requirements are no longer in force. With over 30,000 doctoral dissertations written in the United States each year, it would be both impossible and impractical to attempt to put them all into the hands of the reading public.

At the same time, it is as vital as ever that good dissertations be published and made available to a larger readership. An open enterprise that transcends most boundaries, scholarship can continue to advance only when knowledge is shared and results verified.

There are, moreover, personal satisfactions in having one's thesis published by a reputable company. Direct financial gain should probably be considered as incidental, for it is apt to be negligible. If the author remains in academe, however, the indirect rewards can be more substantial, since publication helps to strengthen a claim to promotion and tenure. For that matter, in any field of employment, a creditable book or article based on the thesis will appear to advantage in one's dossier.

How many dissertations are published each year? The number that appear in book form admittedly is not large. As articles for periodicals or chapters of books, the total is somewhat higher. In examining some 3,012 dissertations written between 1934 and 1969 in sociology, psychology, biology, and education, Moore (1972) found that her sample, although not random, represented about 1 percent of the 288,369 dissertations listed in *American Doctoral Dissertations* for that period. During this same thirty-five-year span, about 2 percent of the dissertations were published as books or government documents, and approximately another 17 percent appeared as journal articles or parts of books. The final decade, 1960–1969, saw the rate of publication dwindle slightly to about .7 percent for books and 12.4 percent for articles. At first glance this figure may be discouraging, but when the percentage is translated into number, the total is more impressive. Assuming Moore's sample is representative, it would appear that more than 200 books and several thousand articles published annually began as dissertations. In addition, one can assume that many papers presented at conventions of scholarly associations were based on recently completed theses.

Dissertation into Book

Why are so few dissertations converted into books? The answer probably lies in the nature of dissertation work, which is an exhaustive scholarly treatment of a subject that may be highly technical, specialized, and even arcane, couched in technical terms or the jargon of a particular discipline. The writing may be abstruse, even pedantic, replete with words and phrases that betray its origin as an exercise in scholarship.

In an interesting collection of essays entitled *The Thesis and the Book* (Harman and Montagnes, 1976), one author observes: "The thesis or dissertation, prepared as a part of a program of graduate study, is only rarely publishable as a book and even more rarely as a good one. On the other hand, many books, and some good ones, have had their origins in dissertations or have been developed from research undertaken for a doctorate" (p. iii). In this same work, a number of other authors, including several editors of university presses, give advice on what is required if a dissertation is to be transformed into a good book.

For firsthand advice on this subject, I turned to three

former students whose dissertations were published as books, and in addition sought advice from two publishers. Their responses are distilled below.

First, it is clear that a dissertation is rarely, if ever, ready for publication in its original form. Indeed, one publisher was blunt: "Dissertations and theses are really not suitable for publication." If that is true, how is it some are published? All three students told me their dissertations were published only after extensive editing and revision. For one author a full seven years separated the acceptance of the dissertation and the publication of the book.

This student has unusually pithy advice. The first step, he says, is to get a publisher to look at your work. It helps if a professor or professors who are well known to the editors of the press will serve as your strong advocates. Your credibility will be further enhanced, he adds, if you publish an article based on your dissertation before you submit your revised manuscript. An article in print will lend some credence to your ability as a scholar; even if the manuscript is still unsuitable for publication, little time will have been lost, and you can get on to other research and scholarly projects.

It must be said, too, that economic factors play a heavy role in publishing—indeed, a crucial role for commercial houses. University presses try to break even if they can; and if they cannot, they try to minimize their losses. The books and scholarly journals published by university and other not-for-profit presses seldom enjoy a wide readership, and a best-seller such as Norman Maclean's semiautobiographical *A River Runs Through It*, published by the University of Chicago Press in 1976, is exceptional. While presses are interested in publishing the best scholarship, they are also interested in remaining solvent. Publication of a raw dissertation in need of heavy revision—one that promises a limited readership and meager sales—is not a salutary prospect for the editor of a university press, much less the editor of a commercial publishing house. Since no publisher is indifferent to the costs of publication, anything you can do to limit outlay will be welcome. If, for example, you can find a person or an institution keenly interested in the subject of your dissertation and willing to subsidize publication, your chances of finding a publisher may increase significantly.

I fear that much of what I have written on this topic is so discouraging that you will conclude there is no hope of publication. I am pleased to report, therefore, that one of the students from whom I asked advice was invited to submit her dissertation to a university press because its editors had heard about the quality of her scholarship from several faculty members. She said she found the process of additional research and revision enjoyable, in part because she was no longer under the time constraints faced by most doctoral students. Her experience, gratifying as it was, is surely atypical.

Some university presses actively discourage freshly minted Ph.D.s from forwarding their dissertations for review. Therefore, anyone who contemplates doing so should carefully scrutinize the manuscript and remove all constructions characteristic of this type of writing. Holmes (1976, p. 54) recommends, for example, the removal of all traces of the "trumpeter effect"—notices, signposts, and reminders such as "This chapter will deal with . . ." and "The last chapter summarizes. . . ." Forewarnings and recapitulation are further evidence of this style. Also to be avoided is the "apologetic opening," or a lengthy statement of reasons why certain things have not been done, sometimes referred to as the "delimiting phenomenon" (p. 56).

Holmes also advises writers to delete excessively repetitious textual matter, and adds: "Some of the signs of still undigested research are too many tables and graphs, an overabundance of footnotes, lengthy bibliographies, a rash of cross-references, and excessive listing" (p. 65). Expressions such as "The investigator found . . ." and "A survey of the literature revealed . . ." and "Everything else being equal . . ." mark a manuscript as the work of a scholar using the jargon of academe, perhaps in an effort to impress the members of his committee.

Davis and Parker (1979) recommend a sharp reduction, or even elimination, of the review-of-the-literature section, as well as fewer subdivisions in the narrative, when the thesis is revised for possible publication. Nevertheless, like many other authorities who cite the dissertation's flaws in this context, Davis and Parker recognize its potential worth as a basis for a serious book. If you are capable of honestly assessing the appeal of your topic, ruthlessly removing those aspects of your work that smack of the academic exercise, and earnestly seeking out the right publisher, there may be a chance for publication.

Finding a Publisher

When the revision is complete, you must decide where to submit your manuscript. A commercial publishing house? One that specializes in textbooks or other scholarly materials? A university or regional press? Obviously, you will need to be selective. If you decide that your best chances lie with a university press, for example, you can consult a current edition of a writer's guide or a list of university and other scholarly presses, such as the *International Directory of Scholarly Publishers* (1977) or *The Association of American University Presses Directory* (1989–). Of the more than one hundred university and other scholarly presses in the United States, you may find half a dozen or so whose publication lists are weighted toward your area of research. For practical purposes, your inquiries should probably begin with these examples. You should not rule out a press because of its limited output, however. An enterprise that publishes only a few books a year may be the very one to accept your manuscript.

The guides to writers' markets, whether general or scholarly, should give such essential information as the address, the name of the editor, the number of books published annually, and the categories of specialization. They should also indicate the form in which the manuscript is to be submitted. Some publishers want an outline and a couple of chapters; others may wish to see the entire manuscript. Most insist that it be accompanied by a stamped, self-addressed envelope.

How long can you expect to wait for a decision on your manuscript? As long as four months—sometimes longer—is not uncommon. If it is accepted, you will probably be asked to sign a publishing contract and will also be informed of royalty arrangements. Practices on this matter vary. University presses, for example, experience the same publication costs of the commercial publishers, but their books tend to appeal to a more limited audience, many selling only a few hundred copies. Consequently, they may pay no royalties until a specified number of copies have been sold, perhaps a thousand. A certain percentage of the purchase price may then be paid on all subsequent sales.

The Thesis as Journal Article

In many cases you will have to face the fact that your dissertation is unsuitable for publication in book form. It may be too short or too long; it may require too many expensive illustrations or printing techniques; it may represent a form of genius that a publisher with an eye to sales will fail to recognize or appreciate; or it may simply have too limited an appeal to warrant book-length treatment.

The results of much doctoral research can often be more appropriately presented as one or more journal articles. With this in mind, you should survey the various journals in your own or closely allied fields. The *Directory of Publishing Opportunities* (1979) lists 3,400 specialized and professional journals by discipline. For each journal it supplies the sponsoring organization's name, address, and telephone number; provides subscription data; indicates the types of articles published, their approximate length, and the audience for which they are intended; and gives information on the submission and disposition of manuscripts. In addition, each issue of a journal usually tells prospective authors how to submit manuscripts for consideration.

Once you have identified some promising markets, you should send a note of inquiry or submit the entire manuscript, bearing in mind the editor's stated preference. Obviously, it will be harder to break into print in the journals that publish only three or four articles (amid dozens of book reviews) each quarter. Some editors who reject a manuscript are good about making suggestions for improvement, however; others may dictate certain changes as a condition of acceptance. In any case, it will be worth a try.

Ethical Problems of Authorship

An ethical problem may emerge when the dissertation is published or an article based on it is accepted by a scholarly journal. Should your faculty adviser be credited as joint author? Some advisers wish to be so listed, especially when they feel they have made a substantial contribution of some kind; others disagree, content to let the dissertation appear as an independent piece of scholarship on the part of the dissertation writer. However, if the dissertation is part of a larger research project, the work of the other authors must be acknowledged in any published articles or reports.

Presenting the Convention Paper

The annual meeting or convention of the scholar's professional association provides an ideal forum for sharing the thesis results with a receptive audience. It should be a simple matter to prepare a twenty- to thirty-minute presentation while the discipline of thesis writing is still strong. For that matter, much of the groundwork will have already been done if an abstract has been written for *Dissertation Abstracts International*.

The appropriate professional journals should be scanned for announcements or "calls for papers," inviting scholars to submit applications to speak at their regional or national convention. Calls for papers usually are accompanied by instructions on how to characterize the research: the research question asked, the techniques employed, the outcomes, and the like.

A few suggestions on presenting the paper follow:

1. Be conscientious in furnishing preliminary copies requested by those responsible for the smooth flow of the convention program. It will ease their burden.
2. Be scrupulous in observing time limits set for program participants.
3. Practice reading the paper aloud to determine how much time will be needed; adjust its length accordingly. When

practicing, strive also for effective technique; ask an associate for critical assessment.

4. Well in advance, locate the room in which the paper will be read; become familiar with the physical layout; determine whether needed equipment is adequate and in working order.

5. When taking part in a panel discussion, be courteous and attentive as other participants present their papers or conclusions.

6. In presenting the paper, keep contact with the audience by glancing at them from time to time. Use good expression and enunciation; show enthusiasm and interest in the topic by varying the pitch and modulation of your voice.

7. Be aware of the lapse of time during the presentation, perhaps by placing a watch on the lectern.

8. Don't expect any dramatic reaction from the audience; don't be concerned if they seem ominously quiet. Silence does not necessarily mean a want of interest.

9. In a question-and-answer session, deal with questions as simply as possible. Be patient with questioners who are obviously more interested in voicing their own views than determining those of the speaker.

Presenting the Paper at the Job Interview

Assume that you are one of the finalists for a faculty position at a college or university and have been invited to campus for a day or two to meet faculty, students, and administrators. Assume also that you have been asked to deliver a paper—one hour in length with time for questions—on your research interests and accomplishments.

I have no recommendation on what you should wear or pack in your overnight carry-on luggage. I do have advice, however, on your presentation and will assume that your topic is your dissertation—even though you may not have finished it when you go for the interview.

Consider, first, the people on the campus you are about to visit. Your audience will probably be a mixture of faculty and graduate students. The graduate students will be interested to learn the substance of your doctoral dissertation, to be sure, but they will also be curious about your comportment, hoping to learn something valuable when they, too, are candidates for a job. Above all, both faculty and graduate students want to learn which of the finalists—each of whom is well qualified for the job—has potential to become the best colleague, teacher, and scholar. Because the decision they reach will be based substantially on the papers presented, it is imperative that you make careful preparation. And the first rule of preparation is practice—in private, repeatedly, and later before a group.

Because you have worked on your dissertation for several months or longer, you are thoroughly familiar with it; you may even have presented a short version of it at a local, regional, or national professional meeting. In my opinion, however, the presentation you will give at the campus is more demanding and therefore requires fresh preparation. For one thing, your paper will be longer, and while it is quite permissible to read a short paper at a professional meeting, the job interview requires a different approach. Here you will be judged for your skills as a teacher as well as a scholar. If you do read your paper, which may be a lengthy process, you may find it hard to hold the attention of your audience. Try to master your content so well that you can present it without reading; if you cannot, then practice reading the paper with as much enthusiasm, variation, and eye contact as possible. The trick to reading a paper, even a short one, is to appear not to be reading it.

What parts of your topic should you emphasize? Your research question, of course. You should also give a brief description of the entire research problem. Don't spend much time reviewing the literature; do, however, describe any prominent theories you employed. Plan to spend most of your time discussing the experiments you performed, the interviews you conducted, and the archival holdings you explored, and explaining what you learned as a result. If time allows, indicate what steps later researchers should take and what changes you would make if you were doing the research over again. Be certain to leave time for interrogation, some of which will probably refer to subsidiary questions you explored in the dissertation but not in your remarks. Listen carefully to each question; if you don't know the answer, say so.

An overhead projector can be effective as a device both to clarify certain points and to lend variety; the blackboard can be used effectively, too. However, practice using the overhead projector and the blackboard until you are comfortable with them. Be sure that what you put on the screen and board can be read at the back of the room and that your charts, graphs, and illustrations are simple and uncluttered. A question many in your audience will ask themselves as they listen to you is "Would I like to be this person's student?" Let the audience know you enjoy the opportunity to present the results of your research. Be enthusiastic, and, if you can, use a little humor as well. When you are finished, your audience should conclude that you enjoyed your present scholarship and have plans for important research to occupy your time in years ahead.

Again I emphasize the importance of preparation and practice, including a full rehearsal. I am absolutely convinced that an excellent presentation makes a significant difference when several highly qualified persons are being considered for a single position. Persuade some of your fellow graduate students and your adviser to hear your presentation and make suggestions. If necessary, deliver your lecture a second or third time and work their suggestions into your disquisition. A well-prepared and skillful presentation is the mark of a candidate well qualified for academic employment.

An Accolade for the Dissertation

You may wonder why I am so keen on master's theses and doctoral dissertations, and the people who write them. After all, no one, as far as I am aware, has conducted a systematic study of the full contribution dissertations have made to the advancement of human knowledge. Essays such as that of Alan Porter and his colleagues (1982), who concluded that the dissertation is "far more than a mundane academic hurdle" (p. 478), are not conclusive. Persuasive but also inconclusive are the words of the former Harvard dean Henry Rosovsky: "For future scholars, course performance is not a reliable indicator of long-term success. The thesis is of far greater significance" (1990, p. 152). The fact that several dissertations have been published as prize-winning books — such as those by A. Hunter Dupree, Thomas M. Doerflinger, and David Gardner — is impressive but not incontrovertible.

Nevertheless, until a contrary view is firmly established, I hold to the position that the dissertation is the capstone of the educational process and ought to be retained and improved. In my view, someone who has learned to recognize a serious problem, to cast a solid research question, and to pursue that question with imagination and energy is someone who is prepared to deal with the future — is, in short, someone who has written a dissertation.

I know only too well the true stories of people who have had unpleasant experiences in graduate school. However, I have also heard the warm tributes paid to the dissertation process by successful scholars who, when they had completed their challenging task, were ready to begin their professional careers with increased confidence and whetted skills. I have also heard about the advisers and supervisory committee members who gave powerful encouragement when it was sorely needed: "I had no idea when I was writing my dissertation that it would be excellent preparation for the job I hold. My adviser told me it would be, but I doubted it. Turns out the old codger was right."

As the years slip away, your memories of graduate school will fade. One day with keen apprehension you will take the dissertation off your library shelf and skim through it. Your first reaction will probably be "It has my name on it, but is it really mine? I can't remember writing some of these paragraphs. But, really, it isn't too bad at that. If I were doing it today, of course, I would change some parts of it quite a bit. I wonder why my adviser let me get away with that claim on page 146. Still, for a kid that age it isn't too bad. Not too bad at all." Then, as your memory of people and events threatens to overwhelm you, you will put the manuscript back on the shelf, where it will stay until you take it down again a few years later.

Please forgive me if I close this book on a personal note. A friend, the late Laurence S. Knappen, once told me that the publication of his doctoral dissertation unmistakably influenced the rest of his professional career. What was true for him was true for me and has been true for many scholars. I hope your experience with a thesis or dissertation is as rewarding as Knappen's and mine.

RESOURCES:
SAMPLE PROPOSALS
AND MANUSCRIPT PAGES

A. Sample Proposal:
   Historical Approach
B. Sample Proposal:
   Experimental Approach
C. Sample Pages

A. Sample Proposal: Historical Approach

For a more detailed discussion of the research proposal, see Chapter Four.

Title Page. The title page of the proposal and the completed dissertation are often similar. Many proposals have a short title followed by a colon and a longer title.

Abstract Page. One page is sufficient—for the abstract that accompanies the proposal. For the completed dissertation, however, the abstract required for *Dissertation Abstracts International* is usually less than 350 words, or about one and a half pages, in length. Local practice may dictate still longer abstracts for the completed work.

Research Problem. A good lead paragraph will catch the reader's attention, but to hold that attention you will want to advance a solid reason for undertaking the study.

Research Question. The heart of any proposal, the research question is often the key to successful dissertations.

Subsidiary Questions.

Terms. Every major word in the research question should be defined.

Review of Relevant Research and Theory. Avoid the temptation to recount research that is merely related in some way to the study proposed; instead, try to show how previous researches and theories have prepared the ground for the proposed study.

Procedure. This section of the proposal should tell the reader precisely how the work is to proceed. If necessary, a step-by-step listing of activities should be considered.

Completion Schedule, Trial Table of Contents, and Brief Bibliography. All may be useful.

THE CARNEGIE INSTITUTION OF WASHINGTON, 1901–1904:

ANDREW CARNEGIE, DANIEL GILMAN, AND JOHN BILLINGS

SEARCH FOR THE EXCEPTIONAL MAN

by

JOHN W. WEYGAND

A proposal for a dissertation to be submitted

in partial fulfillment of the

requirements for the degree of

Doctor of Philosophy

University of Washington

19—

Members of the Supervisory Committee:

Fulton Gaines, Chairman
Ann Hazlett
Merritt Osseo
Luther Pinconning
Carver W. Warbo

John W. Weygand
2386 N. E. Adams St.
Seattle, Washington
Telephone: 673-2910

TABLE OF CONTENTS

ABSTRACT

The Carnegie Institution of Washington was founded on January 22, 1902. Within just two years of its founding, five of the institution's present six major research enterprises were begun. In the study proposed here, an attempt will be made to answer the question "How were the fortunes of the Carnegie Institution of Washington influenced during its formative years, 1901-1904, by its chief financial benefactor, Andrew Carnegie; its first president, Daniel C. Gilman; and the chairman of its Board of Trustees, John S. Billings?"

The major research question and the subsidiary questions were suggested by a thesis advanced by Laurence Veysey in 1965 to the effect that in the development of the American universities in the late nineteenth century the most important academic conflicts arose over questions of basic purpose and kinds and degree of control to be exercised by institutional leaders. In this study, then, "basic purpose" is to be inferred from the particulars or major activities of the C.I.W. authorized by the three major figures, as well as their expressed views on purpose. The "influence" of each major figure will be assessed by examination of the control each exerted over major decisions. The method of analysis will be a variant of

"situational analysis," which calls for a series of steps or
procedures based on the several research questions.

Heaviest reliance for evidence in the proposed study
will be placed on primary sources found in four major
collections: the New York Public Library, the Johns Hopkins
University Library, the Library of Congress, and the
archives of the Carnegie Institution of Washington. Internal
and external critical techniques will be employed in the
assessment of documents.

I

THE RESEARCH PROBLEM

Introduction

On the eve of his retirement as the first president of
the Johns Hopkins University, there came to Daniel Coit
Gilman the opportunity to direct the fortunes of an
institution that promised to become the most important
research enterprise in the United States. Moreover, with the
financial backing of the institution's founder, Andrew
Carnegie, who had set aside as an endowment United States
Steel bonds worth ten million dollars, Gilman faced the
refreshing prospect of guiding an institution that was free
of the usual budgetary deficit.

But Carnegie and Gilman were not to be the only
principals in this new adventure: John S. Billings, who was
for many years a member of the United States Surgeon
General's office and by 1901 the director and organizing
genius behind the New York Public Library, was to serve the
new enterprise as chairman of the Board of Trustees during
its formative years.

It is a measure of the feverish activities of the
institution that, by the end of 1904, five of the six

research enterprises that continue to this day were begun:
the Mount Wilson and Palomar Observatories; the Genetics
Research Unit at Cold Spring Harbor, New York; the
Department of Plant Biology at Stanford, California; the
Geophysical Laboratory in Washington, D.C.; and the
Department of Embryology in Baltimore, Maryland. Over the
years the contributions of the Carnegie Institution of
Washington have been varied and many. The institution has
published hundreds of important research papers written by
its own scientists and by scholars in other research
agencies and universities. Contributions to practical
affairs have been made, as well as scholarly findings
designed to uncover the basic nature of the universe.
Improved ceramics, mining methods, hybrid corn, Pyrex glass,
and radar are just a few achievements to which the
institution has contributed in some way.

Clearly, then, any full understanding of the
development of American scholarship and science must include
a detailed knowledge of the growth and contributions of the
Carnegie Institution of Washington during its early years.
Moreover, any understanding of the early years of the
institution must be based on knowledge of the influence
exerted by the three most prominent contributors to the
activities initiated during those first years. On the basis
of my preliminary study, it appears that Carnegie, Gilman,

and Billings were the principal figures in charting the
destiny of the enterprise; however, other figures, such as
Charles D. Walcott, S. Weir Mitchell, Seth Low, Henry
Higginson, and Andrew D. White, contributed to the affairs
of the enterprise.

Besides providing information on the contributions of
the institution, the parts played by several major figures
in making those contributions possible, and the other
influences on the affairs of the institution, the present
study, it is hoped, will test Laurence Veysey's thesis on
the importance of purpose and control in an institution
whose mission is similar to that of a research university.

The Research Question

How were the fortunes of the Carnegie Institution of
Washington influenced during its formative years, 1901–1904,
by its chief financial benefactor, Andrew Carnegie; its
first president, Daniel C. Gilman; and the chairman of its
Board of Trustees, John S. Billings?

Subsidiary Questions

1. What position did each of the three principals
take with regard to the future of scholarship generally and
of scientific scholarship in particular?

2. What view did each principal have of the future
of the institution?

3. Precisely what part did each principal play in

deciding the major questions to come before the Executive
Committee? The Board of Trustees?

4. How did each principal think the C.I.W. should be
controlled and directed?

5. What was it in the experience of each that
contributed to his view of the best means for control and
direction?

6. What were the personal and professional
relationships between each of the three principals? Between
the principals and others influential in the affairs of the
institution?

7. From whom did the principals receive advice?
Charles S. Peirce, Theodore Roosevelt, T. C. Chamberlin, J.
Franklin Jameson, Charles P. Steinmetz, Albert A. Michelson,
Alexander Agassiz, George Hale, and others.

8. What part did other prominent figures play in the
institution's affairs? Men such as Andrew D. White, Charles
D. Walcott, S. Weir Mitchell, and Henry S. Pritchett.

9. By what process were decisions made?

10. What models were available to guide decisions?
Did the principals know, for example, of the workings of the
Smithsonian, the National Academy of Sciences, the Nobel
Prize Committee, the Royal Society, and the like?

11. How did the C.I.W. expend its funds? What changes
were made between 1901 and 1904 in the way funds were
disbursed?

12. How satisfied were the principals (and others) with the way the institution had developed?

13. What relationship was there with the major universities, especially those engaged in research?

14. What was the response of the press and the scholarly community to the institution?

Terms

Formative years: The years 1901 to 1904 are called the "formative years" because in that period the institution assumed tangible form and launched many of its important projects and five of its permanent enterprises.

Fortunes: The word fortunes is used here to include the achievements of the C.I.W., its successes and failures, and the correspondence between those achievements and the institution's major purposes and governing philosophy.

Influence: The "influence" of each major character on the "fortunes" of the C.I.W. will be determined by the extent to which each is able to convert his opinions and attitude on questions of purpose, control, and major undertakings into tangible achievement or policy.

Review of Relevant Research and Theory

The most impressive book dealing with the history of the American university in its formative years between 1865 and 1910 is that of Laurence Veysey, The Emergence of the American University. It is Veysey's contention that "the two

most important types of academic conflict in the late
nineteenth century were over the basic purpose of the new
university and over the kind and degree of control to be
exerted by the institution's leadership."[1] Whether or not
Veysey proves his thesis is, of course, a matter for debate;
that he marshals impressive evidence in support of his
conclusions seems certain.

The Carnegie Institution of Washington, to be sure,
was not a university; however, it did have part of the same
mission—research; if Veysey's thesis is correct, therefore,
one should expect to find in the C.I.W. the same conflict
found in the new universities. Moreover, because the affairs
of the enterprise were to be determined by Carnegie, Gilman,
Billings, and others—persons who had come from the worlds
of academe, business, science, medicine, and government—it
is reasonable to expect some fundamental differences of
opinion on questions of purpose and methods of control.

At this point a word of warning is in order. In work
of this kind, the aim is to find relationships from which
some general or special theory can be extended, qualified,
modified, corrected, or, perhaps, abandoned in favor of some
new theory. However, as Lawrence Stone and his colleagues
point out in Schooling and Society, it is extremely

---

[1]Laurence Veysey, The Emergence of the American University
(Chicago: University of Chicago Press, 1965), p. viii.

difficult to find clear relationships.[2] Nevertheless, the
Veysey theses do provide an excellent point of departure,
and--who can say?--perhaps one day they will constitute a
fully developed and solid special theory on which to base
additional scholarship for this most important portion of
American intellectual history.

In addition to the pivotal work of Veysey, a number of
other primary and secondary sources are of special value to
this work. In 1970 an excellent biography of Andrew Carnegie
by Joseph Frazier Wall appeared to eclipse earlier
biographies such as John K. Winkler's Incredible Carnegie:
The Life of Andrew Carnegie and Burton J. Hendrick's The
Life of Andrew Carnegie. Of course, Carnegie's Autobiography
of Andrew Carnegie will be consulted along with other books
and articles about the benefactor. Emphasis will be placed
in these researches on primary sources, especially those
found in collections such as the Library of Congress with
its extensive holdings of Carnegie papers. There are
biographies of Gilman--one by Abraham Flexner entitled
Daniel Coit Gilman and one by Francisco Cordasco with the
same title. Useful, too, to these studies will be Hugh
Hawkins's Pioneer: A History of The Johns Hopkins
University, in which Gilman's activities are recounted and

---

[2]Lawrence Stone, ed., Schooling and Society (Baltimore:
Johns Hopkins University Press, 1976), p. xi.

analyzed. John Shaw Billings: A Memoir, by Fielding H.
Garrison, will be consulted along with a "Biographical
Memoir of John Shaw Billings" presented to the annual
meeting of the National Academy of Sciences in 1916 by S.
Weir Mitchell.

I will examine, of course, newspapers in New York,
Boston, Washington, Baltimore, Chicago, and elsewhere, as
well as a sample of scholarly and popular journals, among
them the American Journal of Sociology, Annals of the
American Academy of Political Science, Athenaeum, Century
Magazine, Chautauquan, Cosmopolitan, Dial, Education Review,
Engineering Magazine, Forum, Harper's Bazaar, McClure's,
Nation, New England Magazine, North American Review, Popular
Science Monthly, Quarterly Journal of Economics, Scientific
American, Scribner's, Science, American Engineer, and
others.

Although chief reliance will be placed on the primary
sources listed in the "Procedure" section of this proposal
and the literature already cited, I will study the
literature on the history of American higher education,
including John S. Brubacher and Willis Rudy, Higher
Education in Transition, and Frederick T. Rudolph, The
American College and University: A History, as well as the
literature on the history of science, including such works
as A. Hunter Dupree, Science in the Federal Government;

Howard S. Miller, <u>Dollars for Research: Science and Its</u>
<u>Patrons in the Nineteenth Century</u>; and Daniel Kevles, <u>The</u>
<u>Physicists</u>....

II

PROCEDURE

Conceptual Framework

The study I propose is based on a thesis by Laurence
Veysey, who identified fundamental conflicts within American
universities in the late nineteenth century. Predicated on
this thesis is a major research question augmented by
fourteen subsidiary questions suitably modified to fit the
Carnegie Institution of Washington, an institution dedicated
primarily to research. Three pivotal elements—institutional
purpose, financial support, and control of decisions—have
been chosen for special scrutiny. To understand the early
history of the Carnegie Institution of Washington, one must
assess the ability of three major figures to influence each
pivotal element. The three major figures were the founder,
Andrew Carnegie; Daniel C. Gilman, the first president of
the C.I.W.; and John S. Billings, longtime chairman of the
Board of Trustees.

Method of Analysis

Thus, the starting point of the analysis must be the
concrete behavior of the principal actors. The aim is to try
to explain that behavior, and the technique used is a

variant of what has been called "situational analysis,"
developed by Robert Berkhofer.[3]

A number of questions are asked about behavior:

1. What were the major actions?

2. Who were the major actors?

3. What did each actor contribute to the action?

4. What alternative did each actor consider?

5. What result did each actor expect the action to
have?

6. What were the relationships between the actors at
the moment of decision?

7. What influences were brought to bear on each
actor?

8. What experiences, information, energy, skill, and
the like, did each actor bring to each decision? Other
questions are often included in an analysis of this kind:
Was the actor's behavior consistent with his previous
actions? Was he satisfied with the decision-making process?
Did he have a correct view of the role he played? Did he
accommodate the wishes of others?

Because there seem to be no agreed-upon models or
procedures for analyses of this kind, each student to some
extent must begin anew. Situational analysis is related to

---

[3]A Behavioral Approach to Historical Analysis (New York:
Free Press, 1969), pp. 32-44.

the structural and functional analysis models used for the past twenty years and more by scholars. But I believe that there is a serious danger awaiting anyone who asks: "What is the function or structure of an institution?" There is the danger that a function will be taken at face value, and with most institutions, especially those as complex as the C.I.W., function will seldom be obvious. For that matter, even relatively simple tools and devices may have functions that are not obvious. Take, as an example, the shotgun. If the shotgun's function is to propel lead pellets at clay pigeons, birds, varmints, and the like, why are some shotguns so much more expensive than others? Why will one man pay $140 for a double-barreled shotgun when another will pay $800? To be sure, the more expensive gun may be a little better in the sense that it has a device or two that makes the gun more convenient, but usually these refinements are marginal and do not justify the much higher price. The answer to the mystery lies in an understanding of the complexity of function. The fact is that the shotgun's function is not simple: some people are more interested in the appearance of a shotgun than they are in its pellet-propelling capability. These people prefer a model with a hand-carved stock and etched receiver. Other people buy a gun never intending to shoot it, but instead intending to

display it in a gun case or weapons cabinet. Still others
want a shotgun as insurance against burglars.

There are other pitfalls with the functional
approach—pitfalls that can lead to errors in cause-and-
effect reasoning; but I will not go into them here. Suffice
it to say that I intend to try to see the C.I.W. as a
whole—to see it, perhaps, as a symbol of an ideal. Possibly
the institution was a part of the powerful, and imperfectly
understood, "progressive spirit" abroad in the land in the
early twentieth century. I propose always to keep the
broader implications of the institution in mind as an
antidote to the tendency to reduce the research task to a
few mechanical operations.

Sources of Evidence

As I pointed out above, there are two major sources
for this study. The first, that of secondary materials, has
already been discussed under the "Relevant Research and
Theory" section of this proposal. The second source, and the
one on which major emphasis will be placed, is that of
documents found in certain archives as follows:

1. Andrew Carnegie papers at the Library of Congress
2. Daniel C. Gilman papers at the Johns Hopkins University
   Library
3. John S. Billings papers at the New York Public Library
4. Andrew D. White papers at Cornell University

5. Charles D. Walcott papers at the Smithsonian Institution

6. The Carnegie Institution of Washington collection of

    documents, personal papers, reports, and transcripts of

    Trustee meetings and Executive Committee meetings

Completion Schedule

Jan. 1–Apr. 1 Preliminary study: read biographies of
Carnegie, Gilman, Billings, White,
Mitchell, and others. Search for other
references to C.I.W. examine all
published material available in
university's library.

Apr. 1–June 7 Work in libraries as
follows:

New York Public	5	days
Cornell	2	"
Johns Hopkins	8	"
Library of Congress	2	"
C.I.W.	30	"
Travel	6	"
Other	15	"

June 8–Aug. 31 Analyze evidence.

Sept. 1–Oct. 1 Write first draft.

Oct. 1–Nov. 1 Write second draft.

Nov. 1–Nov. 15 Polish and type.

Nov. 16 Give copy to adviser.

Dec. 15 Get copy back from adviser.

Dec. 15–Jan. 15 Rewrite and polish.

Jan. 15 Give new copy and abstract
to committee members.

Feb. 15 Get comments back from
committee members.

Feb. 15–Mar. 15 Rewrite and polish.

Mar. 15   Give final copy to typist.

Apr. 15   Get final draft from typist.

May 15   Take oral examination.

May 25   Give final copies to
                       committee members, thesis
                       secretary, library,
                       microfilm, and the like.

III

TRIAL TABLE OF CONTENTS

CHAPTER

B. Sample Proposal: Experimental Approach

I am grateful to Kathleen Allard Liberty for permission to use this slightly edited, and shortened, version of her dissertation proposal.

Notice that in this proposal the method of documentation is different from the footnote method used in the preceding proposal. It is a method especially suited to work in which periodicals are used; however, it has limitations for the scholar who uses a variety of sources.

AN INVESTIGATION OF TWO METHODS OF ACHIEVING COMPLIANCE

WITH THE SEVERELY HANDICAPPED IN A CLASSROOM SETTING

by

KATHLEEN ALLARD LIBERTY

A proposal for a dissertation to be submitted

in partial fulfillment of the requirements

for the degree of

Doctor of Philosophy

University of Washington

1977

SUMMARY

By means of two experiments employing a multiple baseline design, I propose to analyze compliance, stereotyped behavior, and performance on an instructional task. My subjects will be six children—ages 6 to 10—three of whom have been labeled severely retarded and three labeled autistic. In the first experiment, three subjects (two autistic and one severely retarded) will receive a "short session" in compliance training at the beginning of each day. During the short sessions, to last ten trials each, compliance will be consequated with praise and food, and noncompliance will be consequated with a physical guidance procedure. Compliance will be measured both during the short session and in the subjects' classroom. In another phase of this study, contingencies identical to those used in the short sessions will be used by the classroom staff throughout the school day, whenever a compliance request is made.

In the second experiment, identical all-day contingencies for compliance will be instituted immediately following baseline for the second group of three subjects, two of whom are severely retarded and one, autistic.

I

THE RESEARCH PROBLEM

Introduction

Handicapped children have been placed in a variety of
environments, ranging from regular classes with supportive
services to totally separate educational and residential
institutions. Decisions as to program placement for the
mildly handicapped have usually considered the possibility
of eventually mainstreaming or integrating the student into
a full-time regular class setting. However, programs for the
more severely handicapped have tended to be in separate,
special, facilities—perhaps because for many years classes
for these students were available only in residential
institutions. Traditionally, little if any consideration has
been given to placing the severely handicapped student with
normal children. Still, recent federal legislation (P.L.
94-142) provides that handicapped children be educated in
environments as close as possible to the educational
settings experienced by normal children. Each successive
move away from full-time regular class placement is seen as
introducing or providing for more environmental and,
perhaps, more educational restriction (Schipper, Wilson, &
Wolfe, 1977)....

Some behaviors which critically affect placement
change have been identified. One class of behavior which has

been of concern to both educators and parents can colloquially be identified as "minding." More specifically, does the child do what he is asked or directed to do? In the literature, "minding"—or responding to adult requests where the child is capable of responding—has been called "compliance." Researchers initially began investigating compliance because commands are commonly used to manage behavior in classroom and home situations (e.g., O'Leary, Baker, Evans, & Saudergas, 1969). Children who do not respond to such commands or instructions present "problems" to their teachers and parents. Such problems may result in special class placement or institutionalization—placements which may be considered more restrictive under the law.

In my paper I shall examine the research conducted on compliance and other related behaviors and conduct a study in which the effects of two different compliance programs will be investigated. Both compliance programs will be conducted in a classroom setting with severely handicapped subjects. In both, the consequences for compliance will be praise plus food, and the consequences for noncompliance will be a complete physical assist to perform the requested response. However, during one study, only short sessions of ten trials' duration will be scheduled, while in the second study, each occurrence of a response or nonresponse to a compliance command during the entire school day will be consequated....

The Research Question

It is the purpose of this study to compare two different approaches—short sessions (massed trial) and all-day sessions (naturally distributed trials)—in an effort to discover which has greater influence in the development of compliance, stereotyped behavior, and performance in the severely handicapped.

Subsidiary Questions

1. Will consequating compliance and noncompliance during a short classroom session improve general classroom compliance?

2. Will consequating compliance and noncompliance each time an instruction is given improve general classroom compliance?

3. Which methods will produce greater change?

4. Will changes in the amount of time subjects engaged in stereotyped behavior be influenced by these treatments?

5. Will these two types of compliance programs affect performance on instructional tasks?

Review of the Literature

The compliance situations investigated have generally followed a basic pattern: the command or direction is given, the response occurs (or does not occur) within an allowable time period, and the consequence for the compliant or

noncompliant response is presented. Various types of
antecedent stimuli and consequences have been tried and
manipulated in the quest for compliance. All of the command-
response pairs investigated were in the repertoire of the
subjects prior to the start of any investigation of
compliance.

Researchers have utilized two basic types of
antecedent stimuli: direct commands and imitative commands.
Direct commands or directions for the behavior are verbal
stimuli such as "Stand up," "Touch your nose," "Clap your
hands," "Look at me," etc. (e.g., Whitman, Zakaras, &
Chardos, 1971; Forehand & King, 1974). Imitative commands or
directions for the behavior are verbal stimuli such as "Do
this," followed by a model or demonstration of the behavior
by the experimenter (e.g., Streifel, Bryan, & Aikins, 1974;
Baer & Sherman, 1964; Peterson, Merwin, Moyer, & Whitehurst,
1971).

In most studies, the experimenters have established a
set time period by which the child must begin responding
before either another trial is presented or the consequence
for nonresponding is implemented. In none of the
investigations studied was a reason given for the choice of
an allowable latency. Five seconds was the selection of the
majority of experimenters (39%) (e.g., Streifel et al.,
1974), while 27% selected ten seconds (e.g., Steinman,

1970b). The longest time reported, thirty seconds, was used
in a regular preschool classroom (Goetz, Holmberg, &
LeBlank, 1975).

Consequences for compliant performance of appropriate
behaviors fall into the two basic categories of social and
primary reinforcers. Social reinforcers, such as praise or
contingent teacher attention, were used alone in about 40%
of the studies (e.g., Schutte & Hopkins, 1970), while food
(e.g., Streifel & Wetherby, 1973) and tokens (e.g., Peterson
& Whitehurst, 1971) were each used in about 20% of the
studies. Other consequences for correct behaviors included
music (Streifel et al., 1974), and combinations of food plus
praise (e.g., Martin, 1971). When investigating the
generalization of compliance, experimenters did not
reinforce every correct response, as will be discussed
later. However, reinforcement always followed compliance to
the appropriate discriminative stimulus. During the
acquisition of compliance, only one-to-one (CRF) schedules
of reinforcement have been utilized.

Consequences for noncompliance have most typically
been timeout, ignoring, or a physical guidance procedure.
Ignoring has been used in the majority of reported studies
(e.g., Steinman, 1970b; Homme, deBaca, Devine, Steinhorst, &
Rickert, 1963), wherein the failure of the child to respond
within the allowable latency period has merely been followed

by the presentation of the next command. Timeout for noncompliance involves the physical removal of the child from the opportunity to receive reinforcement for a set period of time (Budd, Green, & Baer, 1976). Physical guidance involves manipulating, or mandating, the child's performance of the desired behavior (e.g., Whitman et al., 1971; Waxler & Yarrow, 1970). In two studies (Whitman et al., 1971; Baer, Peterson, & Sherman, 1967), the physical guidance procedure was gradually faded.

All studies have used similar measures of compliance. A response is considered correct (compliant) if it is the appropriate response to the command and compliance is initiated within the allowable period. A response is considered incorrect (noncompliant) if (1) it is an incorrect response to the direction or (2) compliance is not initiated within the allowable period. Trials begin with the presentation of the command. Compliance is calculated by dividing the total number of complied or correct trials by the total trials or opportunities to comply and multiplying by 100. Thus, if a subject were given ten opportunities to comply and responded correctly to two of them, he would be considered to be 20% compliant during that session.

Generalization is almost always tested following the acquisition of stimulus control to some predetermined level....

II

PROCEDURE

The studies will be conducted simultaneously with six subjects, utilizing a multiple baseline design. In each study, data will be collected on compliance, stereotyped behavior, and performance on an instructional task. Following baseline in the first study, the three subjects will receive short sessions, compliance will be consequated with praise plus food, and noncompliance will result in a physical guidance procedure. Compliance will be measured both during the short sessions and during regular classroom activities. Following the short session phase, identical contingencies will be applied throughout the day whenever a compliance command is given by a staff member (all-day phase). In the second study, following baseline, compliance to commands will be given during the school day to the three other subjects, who will be consequated with praise plus food, and noncompliance will result in the physical guidance procedure (all-day phase). All procedures will be conducted in the subjects' classroom and implemented by the classroom staff. The following sections detail the procedures.

Subjects

The subjects are six children enrolled in a primary classroom at the Experimental Education Unit (EEU), Child

Development and Mental Retardation Center of the University
of Washington. All six subjects had been referred to the EEU
by their school districts. All children had been placed in
the same classroom because their behavior was considered
"disordered," and constituted the major impediment to
education within their home school districts.... Each of the
six subjects had been classified as severely handicapped by
his or her school district....

Identification of Behaviors

Prior to the first experimental day, the experimenter
and Teachers 1 and 2 will identify compliance commands for
each subject. According to the teachers, each command will
be one to which the subject could comply. A compliant
response to each command will be recorded during the course
of the study. No other verification of whether or not the
subject can perform the response when requested will be
made. These commands will constitute the "pool" for the
study for Subjects 1-5. Each of these commands will request
a motor response (i.e., "Stand up"). Motor commands will
also be identified for Subject 6. However, the teachers will
be most concerned with the compliance to requests for verbal
responses of Subject 6. Beginning on the seventh
experimental day, therefore, compliance data will be also
collected on compliance to requests for verbal responses for

Subject 6. Compliance commands for each subject will be
detailed in an Appendix.

Basic Design

The low density and high heterogeneity of the severely
handicapped population create insoluble problems in
attempting group designs; thus, both experiments will be
single-subject designs, replicated across two other subjects
in each study. The multiple baseline design of single-
subject research allows for replication of procedures across
individuals (Hall, Cristler, Cranston, & Tucker, 1970) while
controlling for some extraneous variables (e.g., history) by
showing that specific changes are associated with the
intervention at different points in time (Kazdin & Kopel,
1975). In this design, the behavior of two or more subjects
is measured simultaneously prior to instituting experimental
procedures. An experimental procedure is then introduced for
one of the subjects. At subsequent points, the procedure is
instituted for the second, then for the third, and so on
(Baer, Wolf, & Risley, 1968).

In Experiment 1, the first experimental procedure
following baseline will be "short sessions" of compliance
training. This will be introduced first for Subject 1, then
for Subject 2, and finally for Subject 3. A period of
several days will separate the application of procedures

from one subject to the next. The "short-session" phase will
be followed by an "all-day compliance training" phase, with
the introduction of these procedures similarly staggered. In
Experiment 2, the baseline phase will be followed by the
introduction of the "all-day" procedures. These also will be
applied at different points in time. Subjects 4 and 5 will
begin the all-day procedures at the same time as Subjects 1
and 2 of the first experiment, respectively, while Subject 6
will begin the procedures at the same time as Subject 3 of
the first experiment. The order of presentation of the
phases is illustrated in Figure 1 and discussed in detail in
the following sections.

Throughout the study, phase lengths will be set so
that: (1) sufficient data are available for meaningful trend
analysis, (2) changes do not occur at the start of a school
week, and (3) the study can be accomplished during one
school quarter.

Experiment 1

Baseline. During baseline, the compliance of Subjects
1, 2, and 3 will be recorded (data collection procedures are
described in a following section). No changes will be made
in the subjects' programs or the general classroom
procedures during this phase.

Experimental Days

1 2 3 4 5 6 7 8 9 10 11 12 13 14 15 16 17 18 19 20 21 22 23 24 25 26 27 28 29 30 31 32 33 34

(S₁) B————————B SS————————SS A————————————————————————————————A

(S₂) B————————————————————B SS————————SS A————————————————————A

(S₃) B————————————————————————B SS————————SS A————————————A

(S₄) B————————————————————————————B A————————————————A

(S₅) B————————————————————————————————B A————————————A

(S₆) B——B A————A

Figure 1. Basic design of Experiment 1 (Subjects 1, 2, 3) and Experiment 2 (Subjects 4, 5, and 6). Baseline days are denoted by "B," days in which the "short-session" procedures will be in effect are labeled "SS," and days in which contingencies for compliance will be in effect all day are labeled as "A." Only school days are shown.

Short session. Beginning on the tenth day for Subject
1, on the fourteenth day for Subject 2, and on the
seventeenth day for Subject 3, short compliance sessions
will be held during the first half hour of the school day.
No compliance commands will be given to the subject prior to
the short session. Ten commands will be randomly selected
each day from the pool of compliance commands for each
subject. The teacher will conduct all short sessions with
each subject. The teacher first will put the commands in the
order in which she will give them and then issue the first
command. If the subject (1) begins to respond to the request
within five seconds and (2) correctly performs the requested
behavior, the subject will be given food (raisins or
peanuts) and praised. If the subject (1) does not begin to
respond to the request within five seconds and/or (2) does
not correctly perform the requested behavior, the teacher
physically will guide the subject through the behavior. The
procedures selected have been used by other researchers, and
their effectiveness has been documented as described in the
review of the literature (e.g., Streifel & Wetherby, 1973;
Baer et al., 1967; Waxler & Yarrow, 1970). The teacher
physically will stop any stereotyped behavior exhibited by
the subject prior to (1) giving the command and/or (2)
consequating the subject. Following each trial, a five- to

ten-second rest period will be in effect. A request for
another behavior will then be given....

Data Collection Procedures

Data on classroom compliance. Data on compliance in
the general classroom setting will be collected daily by
Experimenter 1. A compliance trial will be initiated by a
teacher request for one of the behaviors identified in the
"pool" for that subject. A correct response will be recorded
if (1) the subject began to respond to the request within
five seconds and (2) the subject correctly performs the
requested behavior. An incorrect response will be recorded
if (1) the subject does not begin to respond to the request
within five seconds and/or (2) the subject does not
correctly perform the requested behavior or, for Subject 6,
gives the wrong reply to a command for a verbal response. A
sample of at least ten trials will be collected each day for
each subject. No more than five consecutive trials of the
same command for any given subject will be recorded, so that
the data will represent general compliance to a variety of
commands.

Data on teacher responses to compliance/noncompliance
also will be recorded for each compliance trial. Categories
and definitions are:

1. Repeats: verbal repetition of compliance command prior to compliance/noncompliance of the subject.

2. Praise: verbal praise of the subject following a response (either compliance or noncompliance).

3. Food: presentation of food or drink to the subject following a response (either compliance or noncompliance).

4. Praise + Food: verbal praise and the presentation of food or drink following a response (either compliance or noncompliance).

5. Prompt: a physical gesture, movement, or assist given to the subject prior to the response.

6. Physical Guidance: physically guiding the subject through or to complete the requested behavior.

The occurrence of one or more of these teacher behaviors will be recorded for each trial.

None of the data collected during the course of the study will be shared with the classroom teachers prior to the conclusion of the study. The teachers will, however, have access to the data they collect during the short sessions and the sorting programs.

Reliability checks of the data collected on compliance will be taken on eight different experimental days. During these checks, the second experimenter will collect data on compliance at the same time as Experimenter 1.

1. Reliability on the occurrence of a compliance
    trial will be calculated by dividing the total
    agreements on occurrence by the total agreements
    plus disagreements and multiplying by 100. See
    Sample Table 1.

2. Reliability on the subject to whom the command is
    given and the specific command given will be
    calculated in the same manner.

3. Reliability on whether the response of the subject
    to the command constituted compliance or
    noncompliance also will be calculated.

4. Reliability on the teachers' behavior following
    the command will be calculated three different
    ways. In the first method, both the occurrence and
    nonoccurrence of a given behavior (e.g., repeating
    the command) will be considered an agreement....

An Estimate of the Work Schedule

Preliminary study and reading	June–Dec. 1976
Being intensive reading	Jan. 1, 1977
Complete most of reading	Mar. 1, 1977
Begin proposal writing	Mar. 1, 1977
Proposal draft to two committee members	May 1, 1977
Rewrite proposal	May 1, 1977
Copies of proposal to committee	May 15, 1977

Sample Table 1. Reliability of Data Collected on Compliance.

Day	Occurrence of a Compliance Trial		Identification of Subject and Command		Compliance/Noncompliance to Command	
	Agree/Disagree	Reliability*	Agree/Disagree	Reliability*	Agree/Disagree	Reliability*
5						
8						
9						
14						
15						
21						
26						
34						

*Agreements divided by agreements plus disagreements × 100.

Final approval of proposal by committee	June 1, 1977
(Vacation from dissertation. Very important.)	June 1–20, 1977
Begin data collection	June 21, 1977
Begin rewrite first three chapters	July 1, 1977
End data collection	Aug. 10, 1977
End rewrite first three chapters to two members of committee	Aug. 10, 1977
Begin data analyses	Aug. 10, 1977
End data analyses	Sept. 1, 1977
Begin writing results/discussion	Sept. 1, 1977
Draft completed	Sept. 20, 1977
Draft typed by	Oct. 1, 1977
To Reading Committee	Oct. 1, 1977
Begin rewrite	Oct. 20, 1977
Complete rewrite	Oct. 25, 1977
Reading Committee report to Dean	Nov. 1, 1977
Typed by	Nov. 1, 1977
To full committee	Nov. 2, 1977
Defense	Nov. 22, 1977
Due in graduate office by	Dec. 1, 1977

III

TRIAL TABLE OF CONTENTS

IV

BIBLIOGRAPHY

Ayllon, T., & Azrin, N. H. Reinforcement and instructions
    with mental patients. Journal of Experimental Analysis
    of Behavior, 1964, 1, 327–331.

Baer, D. M., Peterson, R. F., & Sherman, J. A. The
    development of imitation by reinforcing behavioral
    similarity to a model. Journal of Experimental
    Analysis of Behavior, 1967, 10, 405–416.

Baer, D. M., & Sherman, J. A. Reinforcement control of
    generalized imitation in young children. Journal of
    Experimental Child Psychology, 1964, 1, 37–49.

Baer, D. M., Wolf, M. M., & Risley, T. R. Some current
    dimensions of applied behavior analyses. Journal of
    Applied Behavior Analysis, 1968, 1, 91–94.

Bandura, A. Social-learning theory of identificatory
    processes. In D. A. Goslin & D. D. Glass (Eds.),
    Handbook of Socialization Theory and Research.
    Chicago: Rand McNally, 1968.

Baron, A., Kaufman, A., & Stauber, K. A. Effects of
    instructions and reinforcement: Feedback on human
    operant behavior maintained by fixed interval
    reinforcement. Journal of Experimental Analysis of
    Behavior, 1969, 12, 701–712.

Baumeister, A. A., & Forehand, R. Stereotyped acts. In N. R.
Ellis (Ed.), International Review of Research in
Mental Retardation. New York: Academic Press, 1973, 6,
55-96.

Berkson, G., & Mason, W. A. Stereotyped movements of mental
defectives: IV. The effects of toys and the character
of the acts. American Journal of Mental Deficiency,
1964, 68, 511-524.

Brackbill, Y., Adams, G., Crowell, D. H., & Gray, M. L.
Arousal level in neonates and preschool children under
continuous auditory stimulation. Journal of
Experimental Child Psychology, 1966, 4, 178-188.

Bucher, B. Some variables affecting children's compliance
with instructions. Journal of Experimental Child
Psychology, 1973, 15, 10-21.

. . .

C. Sample Pages

1. Title Page
2. Quote Slip
3. Abstract
4. First Page of Chapter
5. Bibliography—A List
6. Essay Bibliography

(Sample Title Page)

THE CARNEGIE INSTITUTION OF WASHINGTON: 1901–1904

by

JOHN W. WEYGAND

A dissertation submitted in partial fulfillment

of the requirements for the degree of

Doctor of Philosophy

University of Washington

19––

Approved by _____

(Chairperson of Supervisory Committee)

Program Authorized to Offer Degree_____

Date_____

(Sample Quote Slip: For more information on the quote slip, see the guide published by your department or graduate school. If a copyright page is included, it should appear after the title page and be unnumbered.)

In presenting this dissertation in partial fulfillment of the requirements for the Doctoral degree at the University of Washington, I agree that the Library shall make its copies freely available for inspection. I further agree that extensive copying of this dissertation is allowable only for scholarly purposes, consistent with "fair use" as specified in the U.S. Copyright Law. Requests for copying or reproduction of the dissertation may be referred to University Microfilms, 300 North Zeeb Road, Ann Arbor, Michigan 48106, to whom the author has granted "the right to reproduce and sell (a) copies of the manuscript in microform and/or (b) printed copies of the manuscript made from microform."

Signature_____

Date_____

(Sample Abstract Page: Usually under 350 words, or about one and a half pages, double spaced. The abstract will appear in Dissertation Abstracts International. *It is not numbered, nor does it appear in the Table of Contents.)*

University of Washington

Abstract

A HISTORY OF THE CARNEGIE INSTITUTION

OF WASHINGTON: 1901-1904

by John W. Weygand

Chairperson of the Supervisory Committee: Professor Fulton Gaines

Within two years of its founding on January 22, 1902, the Carnegie Institution of Washington was well on its way to becoming one of the most important research enterprises of its kind in the world. The research question asked in this dissertation was "How were the fortunes of the Carnegie Institution of Washington influenced during its formative years, 1901-1904, by its chief financial benefactor, Andrew Carnegie; its first president, Daniel C. Gilman; and the chairman of its Board of Trustees, John S. Billings?"

Guided by a thesis put forth by Laurence C. Veysey, I examined major conflicts over purpose and control and employed a technique called "situational analysis" to answer the major research question and the fourteen subsidiary

questions. Whenever possible, I used primary sources,

including the papers of Carnegie, Billings, Gilman, Andrew

D. White, Charles Walcott, and others....

(Sample First Page of Chapter)

CHAPTER I

THE EARLY PROPOSALS

<u>Benjamin Rush and His Plan for a Great University</u>

Dr. Benjamin Rush first recorded his interest in a federal university in a letter to Richard Price on May 25, 1786. He sought, he said, a "federal university under the patronage of Congress" in which "the law of nature and nations, the common law of our country, the different systems of government, history, and everything else connected with the advancement of republican knowledge and principles"[1] were to be taught.

Rush had received his medical training at the University of Edinburgh and, after his return to the colonies, had signed the Declaration of Independence and served as a member of the Continental Congress. During the Revolution he was for a time surgeon-general for the Middle Department, resigning from that position after a disagreement with his superior. After the war Rush helped to found Dickinson College and published essays on prison

---

[1]<u>Letters of Benjamin Rush</u>, ed. L. H. Butterfield (Princeton, N.J.: American Philosophical Society, 1951), I, 388.

(Sample Bibliography: There are at least three ways to present the bibliography: the first is to list the various books, periodicals, and the like, as shown below. The second is to annotate each entry, or, at least, each major entry; and finally, one can provide the reader with an essay on the various major sources, in addition to a list of the minor sources. See an example of the "Essay Bibliography" on page 192.)

BIBLIOGRAPHY

Books

Adams, Charles Francis, ed. Memoirs of John Quincy Adams.

    Vol. VII. Philadelphia: J. B. Lippincott & Co., 1875.

Baker, James H. American University Progress and College

    Reform. New York: Longmans, Green & Co., 1916.

Articles and Periodicals

Boynton, H. V. "Our National University." The Chautauquan,

    IX, 10, July 1889, 569–571.

Congressional Documents

U.S. Senate. "Memorial in Regard to a National University."

    Miscellaneous Document 222. 52nd Cong., 1st Sess.,

    1892.

Congressional Proceedings

U.S. House of Representatives. The Debates and Proceedings

    in the Congress of the United States (Annals of

    Congress). I, 1st Cong., 2nd Sess. Washington, D.C.:

    Gales and Seaton, 1834.

Records and Reports

Kayser, Elmer L. The George Washington University. Records

of the Columbia Historical Society, vols. 53–54.

Washington, D.C.: Columbia Historical Society, 1959.

Unpublished Material

Corson, Louis D. "University Problems as Described in the

Personal Correspondence Among D. C. Gilman, A. D.

White, and C. W. Eliot." Ph.D. dissertation, Stanford

University, 1951.

Other Sources

Ryan, W. Carson, Studies in Early Graduate Education.

Bulletin No. 30. New York: Carnegie Foundation for the

Advancement of Teaching, 1939.

(Sample Bibliography: Another form of the bibliography is the "Essay Bibliography," in which the author discusses the major sources consulted and simply lists the minor sources.)

AN ESSAY BIBLIOGRAPHY

The student interested in the general history of American higher education will find two volumes that complement each other. The first, which appeared in 1958 and was revised in 1968 and again in 1976, is the work of John Brubacher and Willis Rudy and is entitled Higher Education in Transition. The second, published in 1962 and entitled The American College and University: A History, was written by Frederick Rudolph of Williams College. Rudolph's book is delightfully readable and a sound general history, and it contains, moreover, a bibliography that is the best of its kind. The book by Brubacher and Rudy, on the other hand, provides more information on a variety of special topics, and the revised edition affords a lengthy list of college and univerity histories. In addition, Brubacher and Rudy in the last edition have analyzed the momentous events of the 1960s and 1970s in American higher education with considerable skill.

Anyone interested in primary sources assembled in a documentary history, or book of readings, will find several titles from which to choose. One of the best is a two-volume work entitled American Higher Education ...

REFERENCES

Allen, G. R. *Graduate Students' Guide to Theses and Dissertations.* San Francisco: Jossey-Bass, 1973.

American Association of University Professors. "Regulations Governing Research on Human Subjects." *Academe,* 1981, *67,* 358–370.

American Chemical Society. *The ACS Style Guide: A Manual for Authors and Editors.* Washington, D.C.: American Chemical Society, 1986.

American Institute of Biological Sciences. *Council of Biology Editors Style Manual: A Guide for Authors, Editors, and Publishers in the Biological Sciences.* (4th ed.) Arlington, Va.: American Institute of Biological Sciences, 1978.

American Institute of Physics. *Style Manual for Guidance in the Preparation of Papers for Journals Published by the American Institute of Physics.* (3rd ed.) New York: American Institute of Physics, 1978.

American Medical Association. *Style Book and Editorial Manual.* (4th ed.) Chicago: American Medical Association, 1966.

American Psychological Association. *Ethical Principles in the Conduct of Research with Human Participants.* Washington, D.C.: American Psychological Association, 1982.

American Psychological Association. *Publication Manual of the American Psychological Association*. (3rd ed.) Washington, D.C.: American Psychological Association, 1983.

American Statistics Index: A Comprehensive Guide and Index to the Statistical Publications of the U.S. Government. Washington, D.C.: Congressional Information Service, 1973–.

The Association of American University Presses Directory. New York: Association of American University Presses, 1989–.

Baker, S. *The Practical Stylist*. (5th ed.) New York: HarperCollins, 1981.

Balian, E.S. *How to Design, Analyze, and Write Doctoral or Master's Research*. (2nd ed.) Lanham, Md.: University Press of America, 1988.

Ballou, S. V. *A Model for Theses and Research Papers*. Boston: Houghton Mifflin, 1970.

Barford, N. C. *Experimental Measurements: Precision, Error and Truth*. (2nd ed.) New York: Wiley, 1985.

Barr, M. A. "The Selection of a Dissertation Topic: Elements Influencing Student Choice." Unpublished doctoral dissertation, Department of Higher Education, Ohio State University, 1984.

Barrass, R. *Scientists Must Write: A Guide to Better Writing for Scientists, Engineers, and Students*. New York: Wiley, 1978.

Barrass, R. *Students Must Write: A Guide to Better Writing in Course Work*. London: Methuen, 1982.

Barzun, J. *The American University*. New York: HarperCollins, 1968.

Barzun, J. *Simple and Direct: A Rhetoric for Writers*. New York: HarperCollins, 1985.

Barzun, J. *On Writing, Editing, and Publishing: Essays, Explicative and Hortatory*. (2nd ed.) Chicago: University of Chicago Press, 1986.

Barzun, J., and Graff, H. *The Modern Researcher*. (4th ed.) Orlando, Fla.: Harcourt Brace Jovanovich, 1985.

Bassett, C.L.L. "The Doctoral Dissertation: A Study of the Dissertation Experience at the University of Iowa." Unpublished doctoral dissertation, Department of Higher Education, University of Iowa, 1978.

Bauer, D. G. *The "How To" Grants Manual: Successful Grant-Seeking Techniques for Obtaining Public and Private Grants.* New York: American Council on Education and Macmillan, 1984.

Baxter, R. "Effects of Institutionalization on the Social-Psychological Well-Being of the Aged." Unpublished doctoral dissertation, Department of Sociology, Princeton University, 1976.

Becker, H. S. *Writing for Social Scientists: How to Start and Finish Your Thesis, Book, or Article.* Chicago: University of Chicago Press, 1986.

Behling, J. H. *Guidelines for Preparing the Research Proposal.* (Rev. ed.) Lanham, Md.: University Press of America, 1984.

Bell, M. V., and Bacon, J. C. *"Poole's Index": Date and Volume Key. . .* Chicago: Association of College and Reference Libraries, 1957.

Belth, M. *The Process of Thinking.* New York: McKay, 1977.

Benkin, E. M. "Where Have All the Doctoral Students Gone? A Study of Doctoral Student Attrition at UCLA." Unpublished doctoral dissertation, Department of Higher Education, University of California, Los Angeles, 1984.

Benson, L. *Toward the Scientific Study of History: Selected Essays.* Philadelphia: Lippincott, 1972.

Berelson, B. *Graduate Education in the United States.* New York: McGraw-Hill, 1960.

Berkhofer, R. R., Jr. *A Behavioral Approach to Historical Analysis.* New York: Free Press, 1969.

Beveridge, W. I. B. *The Art of Scientific Investigation.* New York: Norton, 1951.

Bibliographic Index: A Cumulative Bibliography of Bibliographies. New York: Wilson, 1938-.

Biography and Genealogy Master Index. Detroit: Gale Research, 1975-.

Biological and Agricultural Index. New York: Wilson, 1964-.

Black, M. *Models and Metaphors.* Ithaca, N.Y.: Cornell University Press, 1962.

Blalock, H. M. *Causal Models in the Social Sciences.* Hawthorne, N.Y.: Aldine, 1985.

Books in Print. New York: Bowker, 1948-.

Boulding, K. *A Primer on Social Dynamics.* New York: Free Press, 1970.

Brodbeck, M. "Models, Meaning and Theories." In L. Gross (ed.), *Symposium on Sociological Theory.* New York: HarperCollins, 1959.

Brodbeck, M. (comp.). *Readings in the Philosophy of the Social Sciences.* New York: Macmillan, 1968.

Brownlee, K. A. *Statistical Theory and Methodology: In Science and Engineering.* (2nd ed.) New York: Wiley, 1984.

Campbell, D. T. *Methodology and Epistemology for Social Science: Selected Papers.* (E. S. Overman, ed.) Chicago: University of Chicago Press, 1988.

Campbell, D. T., and Stanley, J. C. "Experimental and Quasi-Experimental Designs for Research on Teaching." In N. L. Gage (ed.), *Handbook of Research on Teaching.* Skokie, Ill.: Rand McNally, 1963.

Campbell, W. G., and Ballou, S. V. *Form and Style: Theses, Reports, Term Papers.* (8th ed.) Boston: Houghton Mifflin, 1990.

Chicago Guide to Preparing Electronic Manuscripts. Chicago: University of Chicago Press, 1987.

The Chicago Manual of Style. (13th ed.) Chicago: University of Chicago Press, 1982.

Clark, B. R. *The Higher Education System.* Berkeley: University of California Press, 1983.

Clark, B. R. *The Academic Life: Small Worlds, Different Worlds.* Princeton, N.J.: Princeton University Press, 1987.

Cole, A. H., and Bigelow, K. W. *A Manual of Thesis-Writing: for Graduates and Undergraduates.* New York: Wiley, 1946.

Coleman, J. S. *Equality of Educational Opportunity.* Washington, D.C.: U.S. Department of Education, 1966.

Comprehensive Dissertation Index. Ann Arbor, Mich.: University Microfilms International, 1973–.

Cook, C. K. *Line by Line: How to Edit Your Own Writing.* Boston: Houghton Mifflin, 1985.

Cook, T. D., and Campbell, D. T. *Quasi-Experimentation.* Skokie, Ill.: Rand McNally, 1979.

Council of Graduate Schools. *The Doctor of Philosophy Degree: A Policy Statement.* Washington, D.C.: Council of Graduate Schools, 1990a.

Council of Graduate Schools. *Research Student and Supervisor: An Approach to Good Supervisory Practice.* Washington, D.C.: Council of Graduate Schools, 1990b.

Council of Graduate Schools. *The Role and Nature of the Doctoral Dissertation: A Policy Statement.* Washington, D.C.: Council of Graduate Schools, 1991.

Cox, D. R. *Planning Experiments.* New York: Wiley, 1958.

Cox, D. R. *Applied Statistics: Principles and Examples.* New York: Chapman & Hall, 1981.

Daiute, C. *Writing and Computers.* Reading, Mass.: Addison-Wesley, 1985.

Dart, M. "The Effects of Three Prenatal Psychological Interventions on the Course and Outcome of Pregnancy." Unpublished doctoral dissertation, Department of Psychology, Harvard University, 1977.

Davinson, D. *Theses and Dissertations: As Information Sources.* Hamden, Conn.: Linnet Books, 1977.

Davis, G. B., and Parker, C. *Writing the Doctoral Dissertation: A Systematic Approach.* Woodbury, N.Y.: Barron's Educational Series, 1979.

Davis, R. M. *Thesis Projects in Science and Engineering.* New York: St. Martin's Press, 1980.

Dean, J. "An Examination of the Effects of Suburban Growth Controls on Low- and Middle-Income Households in Metropolitan Regions." Unpublished doctoral dissertation, Department of Urban and Regional Planning, Princeton University, 1977.

Directory of Publishing Opportunities. (4th ed.) Chicago: Marquis Academic Media, 1979.

Directory of Research Grants. Phoenix: Oryx Press, 1975–.

Dissertation Abstracts International. Ann Arbor, Mich.: University Microfilms International, 1938–.

Dissertation Handbook: Preparing and Submitting Your Doctoral Dissertation. Ann Arbor: Horace H. Rackham School of Graduate Studies, University of Michigan, 1990.

Dixon, W. J. (ed.). *BMDP: Biomedical Computer Programs.* (3rd ed.) Berkeley: University of California Press, 1973.

Dixon, W. J. *BMDP: Statistical Software.* Berkeley: University of California Press, 1985.

Doerflinger, T. M. *A Vigorous Spirit of Enterprise: Merchants and Economic Development in Revolutionary Philadelphia.* Chapel Hill: University of North Carolina Press, 1986.

Downs, R. B., and Keller, C. D. *How to Do Library Research.* (2nd ed.) Urbana: University of Illinois Press, 1975.

Dupree, A. H. *Asa Gray: 1810–1888.* Cambridge, Mass.: Belknap Press of Harvard University, 1959.

Education Index. New York: Wilson, 1929–.

Engel, M. "Thesis and Antithesis: Reflections on the Education of Researchers in Psychology." *American Psychologist,* 1966, *21,* 781–787.

Enright, J. "The Impact of Presentence Investigation on Plea Bargained Dispositions in Kings County Supreme Court (New York)." Unpublished doctoral dissertation, Department of Sociology, City University of New York, 1987.

Finkelstein, M. J. *The American Academic Professions: A Synthesis of Social Scientific Inquiry Since World War II.* Columbus: Ohio State University Press, 1984.

Fischer, D. H. *Historians' Fallacies: Toward a Logic of Historical Thought.* New York: HarperCollins, 1970.

Forthcoming Books: A Forecast of Books to Come. New York: Bowker, 1966–.

The Foundation Directory. (11th ed.) New York: The Foundation Center, 1987.

Francis, J. B., Bork, C. E., and Carstens, S. P. *The Proposal Cookbook: A Step by Step Guide to Dissertation and Thesis Writing.* (3rd ed.) Buffalo, N.Y.: Action Research Associates, 1979.

Friedenberg, E. Z., and Roth, J. *Self Perception in the University: A Study of Successful and Unsuccessful Graduate Students.* Supplemental Education Monograph no. 80. Chicago: University of Chicago Press, 1954.

Gardner, D. C., and Beatty, G. J. *Dissertation Proposal Guidebook.* Springfield, Ill.: Thomas, 1980.

Gardner, D. P. *The California Oath Controversy.* Berkeley: University of California Press, 1967.

Garson, D. *Academic Microcomputing: A Resource Guide.* Newbury Park, Calif.: Sage, 1987.

Gates, J. K. *Guide to the Use of Libraries and Information Sources.* (6th ed.) New York: McGraw-Hill, 1989.

Girves, J. E., and Wemmerus, V. "Developing Models of Graduate Student Degree Progress." *Journal of Higher Education*, March–April 1988, *59* (2), 165–189.

Glazer, J. S. *The Master's Degree: Tradition, Diversity, Innovation.* Higher Education Report no. 6. Washington, D.C.: Association for the Study of Higher Education, 1986.

Gowers, E. *The Complete Plain Words*. New York: Penguin, 1962.

Grants for Graduate Students. (A. Leskes, ed.) Princeton, N.J.: Peterson's Guides, 1986.

The Grants Register, 1985–1987. (9th ed.) New York: St. Martin's Press, 1984.

Griffiths, C. "The Sources of Variability in Juvenile Court Decision-Making: An Organizational Analysis." Unpublished doctoral dissertation, Department of Sociology, University of Montana, 1977.

Guide for the Care and Use of Laboratory Animals. Publication no. NIH 85-23. Washington, D.C.: U.S. Government Printing Office, 1985.

Hall, M. S. *Getting Funded: A Complete Guide to Proposal Writing*. (3rd ed.) Portland, Oreg.: Portland State University, 1988.

Hamer, P. M. *A Guide to Archives and Manuscripts in the United States*. New Haven, Conn.: Yale University Press, 1961.

Harman, E., and Montagnes, I. (eds.). *The Thesis and the Book*. Toronto: University of Toronto Press, 1976.

Harris, M. B. "Accelerating Dissertation Writing: Case Study." *Psychological Reports*, 1974, *32*, 984–986.

Harvey, J. *The Student in Graduate School*. Washington, D.C.: American Association of Higher Education, 1972.

Heiss, A. M. *Challenge to Graduate Schools*. San Francisco: Jossey-Bass, 1970.

Hesse, M. B. *Models and Analogies in Science*. South Bend, Ind.: University of Notre Dame Press, 1966.

Hobish, T. T. "A Study of Selected Psychological Factors Related to Completion or Non-completion of the Doctoral Dissertation Among Male and Female Doctoral Degree Applicants." Unpublished doctoral dissertation, Department of Psychology, New York University, 1978.

Holmes, O. "Thesis to Book: What to Do with What Is Left." In E.

Harman and I. Montagnes (eds.), *The Thesis and the Book*. Toronto: University of Toronto Press, 1976.

Hull, C. H., and Nie, N. H. *SPSS Update*. New York: McGraw-Hill, 1981.

Humanities Index. New York: Wilson, 1974–.

Index to International Statistics. Washington, D.C.: Congressional Information Service, 1983–.

Index to the [London] Times. London: The Times, 1906–.

Index to U.S. Government Periodicals. Chicago: Infordot International, 1972–.

Irmscher, W. F. *The Holt Guide to English*. New York: Holt, Rinehart & Winston, 1985.

Jones, D. P. (ed.). *Using National Databases*. New Directions for Institutional Research, no. 64. San Francisco: Jossey-Bass, 1989.

Jordan, L. (ed.). *The New York Times Manual of Style and Usage*. (2nd ed.) New York: Times Books, 1982.

Kaplan, M. A. *On Historical and Political Knowing: An Inquiry into Some Problems of Universal Law and Human Freedom*. Chicago: University of Chicago Press, 1971.

Katz, M. J. *Elements of the Scientific Paper*. New Haven, Conn.: Yale University Press, 1985.

Kerlinger, F. N. "The Influence of Research on Educational Practice." *Educational Researcher*, 1977, *6*, 5–12.

Kerlinger, F. N. *Behavioral Research: A Conceptual Approach*. New York: Holt, Rinehart & Winston, 1979.

Kerlinger, F. N. *Foundations of Behavioral Research*. (3rd ed.) New York: Holt, Rinehart & Winston, 1986.

Klecka, W. R., Norusis, M. J., and Hull, C. H. *SPSS Primer*. New York: McGraw-Hill, 1982.

Krathwohl, D. R. *How to Prepare a Research Proposal*. Syracuse, N.Y.: Syracuse University Press, 1977.

Krathwohl, D. R. *Social and Behavioral Science Research: A New Framework for Conceptualizing, Implementing, and Evaluating Research Studies*. San Francisco: Jossey-Bass, 1985.

Kronick, D. A. *The Literature of the Life Sciences: Reading, Writing, Research*. Philadelphia: ISI [Institute for Scientific Information] Press, 1985.

Lamport, L. *LaTex: A Document Preparation System.* Reading, Mass.: Addison-Wesley, 1986.

Langland, B. M. "The Use of Clinical, Laboratory, and Radiology Findings to Predict Admission, Need for Admission, and Surgery in Emergency Room Patients with Abdominal Pain." Unpublished doctoral dissertation, Department of Health Sciences, University of California, Los Angeles, 1987.

Lansbury, P. T. "Selection of Thesis Research: The Most Important Course." *Journal of Chemical Education,* 1975, *52,* 510–511.

Lawler, E. E., III, and Associates. *Doing Research That Is Useful for Theory and Practice.* San Francisco: Jossey-Bass, 1985.

Leedy, P. D. *Practical Research: Planning and Design.* (4th ed.) New York: Macmillan, 1989.

Leggett, G., Mead, D. D., and Charvat, W. *Prentice-Hall Handbook for Writers.* (10th ed.) Englewood Cliffs, N.J.: Prentice-Hall, 1988.

Lester, J. D. *Writing Research Papers.* (5th ed.) Glenview, Ill.: Scott, Foresman, 1987.

Library of Congress — Subject Headings. (12th ed.) Washington, D.C.: Library of Congress, 1988.

Light, R. J., and Pillemer, D. B. *Summing Up: The Science of Reviewing Research.* Cambridge, Mass.: Harvard University Press, 1984.

Light, R. J., Singer, J. D., and Willett, J. B. *By Design: Planning Research on Higher Education.* Cambridge, Mass.: Harvard University Press, 1990.

Lincoln, Y. S., and Guba, E. G. *Naturalistic Inquiry.* Newbury Park, Calif.: Sage, 1985.

Lipshutz, B. "Molecular Oxygen as a Reagent in the Development of New Synthetic Methods." Unpublished doctoral dissertation, Department of Chemistry, Yale University, 1977.

Locke, L. F., Spirduso, W. W., and Silverman, F. J. *Proposals That Work: A Guide for Planning Dissertations and Grant Proposals.* (2nd ed.) Newbury Park, Calif.: Sage, 1987.

Long, T. J., Convey, J. J., and Chwalek, A. R. *Completing Dissertations in the Behavioral Sciences and Education: A Systematic Guide for Graduate Students.* San Francisco: Jossey-Bass, 1985.

Luey, B. *A Handbook for Academic Authors*. New York: Cambridge University Press, 1987.

McCrimmon, J. *Writing with a Purpose*. (9th ed.) Boston: Houghton Mifflin, 1988.

Maclean, N. *A River Runs Through It*. Chicago: University of Chicago Press, 1976.

Mah, D. M. "The Process of Doctoral Candidate Attrition: A Study of the All But Dissertation (ABD) Phenomenon." Unpublished doctoral dissertation, Department of Education, University of Washington, 1986.

Malaney, G. D. "A Decade of Research on Graduate Students: A Review of the Literature in Academic Journals." Paper presented at the annual meeting of the Association for the Study of Higher Education in America, Baltimore, 1987. ERIC Document: ED 292 383.

Mallon, T. *Stolen Words: Forays into the Origins and Ravages of Plagiarism*. New York: Ticknor & Fields, 1989.

Mann, T. *A Guide to Library Research Methods*. New York: Oxford University Press, 1987.

Mauch, J. E., and Birch, J. W. *Guide to the Successful Thesis and Dissertation*. (2nd ed.) New York: Marcel Dekker, 1989.

Maughmer, M. D. "Trailing Edge Flow Conditions as a Factor in Airfoil Design." Unpublished doctoral dissertation, Department of Engineering, University of Illinois, 1984.

Mawdsley, R. D. "Legal Aspects of Plagiarism." Topeka, Kans.: National Organization on Legal Problems of Education, 1985.

Mayhew, L. B. *Reform in Graduate Education*. Monograph no. 18. Atlanta: Southern Regional Education Board, 1972.

Medawar, P. B. *Advice to a Young Scientist*. New York: Harper-Collins, 1979.

Merton, R. K. *Social Theory and Social Structures*. (Enlarged ed.) New York: Free Press, 1968.

Michaelson, H. B. *How to Write and Publish Engineering Papers and Reports*. (2nd ed.) Philadelphia: ISI [Institute for Scientific Information] Press, 1986.

Miller, J. I., and Taylor, B. J. *The Thesis Writer's Handbook: A*

Complete One-Source Guide for Writers of Research Papers. West Linn, Oreg.: Alcove Publishing, 1987.

Miller, K. J. "The Effects of Temperature and Salinity on the Phospholipid and Fatty Acid Composition of a Halotolerant, Psychrotolerant Bacterium Isolated from Antarctic Dry Valley Soil." Unpublished doctoral dissertation, Department of Microbiology, University of Massachusetts, 1984.

Mills, J. S. "Interaction of Calcium, Metal Ions, and Calmodulin Antagonist Drugs and Target Proteins with Calmodulin." Unpublished doctoral dissertation, Department of Chemistry, Ohio State University, 1987.

Modern Language Association of America. *MLA Handbook for Writers of Research Papers, Theses, and Dissertations.* (3rd ed.) New York: Modern Language Association of America, 1988.

Moore, J. L. "Bibliographic Control of American Doctoral Dissertations." *Special Libraries,* 1972, *63* (3), 287–289.

Morgan, G. *Beyond Method: Strategies for Social Research.* Newbury Park, Calif.: Sage, 1983.

Murphy, K. "Ability, Performance, and Compensation: A Theoretical and Empirical Investigation of Managerial Labor Contracts." Unpublished doctoral dissertation, Department of Economics, University of Chicago, 1984.

The National Union Catalog of Manuscript Collections. Washington, D.C.: Library of Congress, 1971 and supps.

New York Times Index. New York: New York Times Co., 1913–.

Norusis, M. J. *SPSS Introductory Guide: Basic Statistics and Operations.* New York: McGraw-Hill, 1982.

Norusis, M. J. *The SPSS Guide to Data Analysis.* Chicago: SPSS Inc., 1988.

Oxford English Dictionary. (2nd ed.) Oxford: Clarendon Press, 1989.

Parsons, P. *Getting Published: The Acquisition Process at University Presses.* Knoxville: University of Tennessee Press, 1989.

Parsons, T., and others (eds.). *Theories of Society.* Vol. 1. New York: Free Press, 1961.

Pelikan, J. *Scholarship and Its Survival: Questions on the Idea of Graduate Education.* Princeton, N.J.: Carnegie Foundation for the Advancement of Teaching and Princeton University Press, 1983.

de Sola Pool, I. "The New Censorship of Social Research." *Public Interest*, 1980, *59*, 57–66.

Poole's Index to Periodical Literature: 1801–1881. (3rd ed. rev.) Boston: Houghton Mifflin, 1891.

Porter, A. L., and others. "The Role of the Dissertation in Scientific Careers." *American Scientist*, 1982, *70*, 475–481.

Powell, W. W. *Getting into Print: The Decision-Making Process in Scholarly Publishing*. Chicago: University of Chicago Press, 1985.

Proctor, J. "An Empirical Analysis of the Effects of State Usury Laws on the Performance of Savings and Loan Associations and Housing Starts in 1974." Unpublished doctoral dissertation, Department of Economics, Clemson University, 1976.

Rashdall, H. *The Universities of Europe in the Middle Ages*. Vol. 1. Oxford: Clarendon Press, 1936. (Originally published in 1895.)

Reader's Guide to Periodical Literature. New York: Wilson, 1900–.

Reid, W. M. "Will the Future Generations of Biologists Write a Dissertation?" *BioScience*, 1978, *28*, 651–654.

Remington, R., and Schork, M. A. *Statistics with Applications in the Biological and Health Sciences*. (2nd ed.) Englewood Cliffs, N.J.: Prentice-Hall, 1985.

Ren, P. "Effects of Coumarin and Indanedione Anticoagulants on Prothrombin Synthesis and Vitamin-K Epoxide Cycle in Normal and Warfarin Resistant Rats." Unpublished doctoral dissertation, Department of Chemistry, University of Rhode Island, 1976.

Rivers, W. L. *Finding Facts: Interviewing, Observing, Using Reference Sources*. Englewood Cliffs, N.J.: Prentice-Hall, 1975.

The Role of the Dissertation in Doctoral Education at the University of Michigan: Summary of the Report of the Dissertation Review Committee. Ann Arbor: Horace H. Rackham School of Graduate Studies, University of Michigan, 1976.

Rondinelli, R. "A Multivariate Morphometric Study of Cranio-Vertebral Shape Changes in Man and Various Nonhuman

Primates." Unpublished doctoral dissertation, Department of Anthropology, University of Illinois, 1977.

Rosovsky, H. *The University: An Owner's Manual.* New York: Norton, 1990.

Ryan, B. F., and Joiner, B. L. *Minitab Handbook.* (2nd ed.) Boston: PWS-Kent, 1985.

Sanford, M. "Making Do in Graduate School." Unpublished doctoral dissertation, Department of Sociology, University of California, Berkeley, 1970.

Schreiner, S. E. "The Theater of His Glory: Nature and the Natural Order in the Thought of John Calvin." Unpublished doctoral dissertation, Department of Religion, Duke University, 1983.

Shaw, P. "Plagiary." *American Scholar*, Summer 1982, pp. 325–337.

Sheehy, E. P. (ed.). *Guide to Reference Books.* (10th ed.) Chicago: American Library Association, 1986.

Smith, R. *Graduate Research: A Guide for Students in the Sciences.* (2nd ed.) New York: Plenum Press, 1990.

Social Sciences Index. New York: Wilson, 1974– .

SPSS, Inc. *SPSS X: A Complete Guide to SPSS Language and Operations.* New York: McGraw-Hill, 1983.

Spurr, S. H. *Academic Degree Structures: Innovative Approaches.* New York: McGraw-Hill, 1970.

Statistical Reference Index. Washington, D.C.: Congressional Information Service, 1980– .

Sternberg, D. *How to Complete and Survive a Doctoral Dissertation.* New York: St. Martin's Press, 1981.

Stock, M. *A Practical Guide to Graduate Research.* New York: McGraw-Hill, 1985.

Storr, R. J. *The Beginnings of the Future: A Historical Approach to Graduate Education.* New York: McGraw-Hill, 1972.

Strong, W. S. *The Copyright Book: A Practical Guide.* (2nd ed.) Cambridge, Mass.: MIT Press, 1984.

Strunk, W., and White, E. B. *The Elements of Style.* (3rd ed.) New York: Macmillan, 1979.

Subject Guide to Books in Print. 2 vols. New York: Bowker, 1988.

Swarz, I. P. "A Historical Investigation of the Impact of World

War II on Harvard Medical School, 1938–1948." Unpublished doctoral dissertation, Department of Education, University of Connecticut, 1983.

Thackrey, D. E. (ed.). *Research: Definition and Reflection.* Ann Arbor: University of Michigan Press, 1967.

Tronsgard, D. T. "A Common-Sense Approach to the Dissertation." *Journal of Higher Education*, 1963, *34*, 491–495.

Tuchman, B. W. *A Distant Mirror: The Calamitous Fourteenth Century.* New York: Knopf, 1978.

Tucker, A., Gottlieb, D., and Pease, J. *Factors Related to Attrition Among Doctoral Students.* Cooperative Research Program (no. 1146) of U.S. Office of Education. East Lansing: Michigan State University, 1964.

Tukey, J. W. *Exploratory Data Analysis.* Reading, Mass.: Addison-Wesley, 1977.

Tullock, G. *The Organization of Inquiry.* Durham, N.C.: Duke University Press, 1966.

Turabian, K. L. *A Manual for Writers of Term Papers, Theses, and Dissertations.* (5th ed. rev.) Chicago: University of Chicago Press, 1987.

A Uniform System of Citation. (14th ed.) Cambridge, Mass.: Harvard Law Review Association, 1986.

U.S. Bureau of the Census. *Statistical Abstract of the United States.* Washington, D.C.: U.S. Government Printing Office, 1878–.

U.S. Government Printing Office. *Style Manual.* (Rev. ed.) Washington, D.C.: U.S. Government Printing Office, 1984.

van Leunen, M. *A Handbook for Scholars.* New York: Knopf, 1978.

Van Til, W. *Writing for Professional Publication.* (2nd ed.) Newton, Mass.: Allyn & Bacon, 1983.

Verplanck, W. S. "An 'Overstatement' on Psychological Research: What Is a Dissertation?" *Psychological Record*, 1970, *20*, 119–122.

Warren, S. L. "Plantation Management: Its Influence on Soil Fertility, Herbaceous Vegetation and Growth of Fraser Fir and Norway Spruce." Unpublished doctoral dissertation, Department of Agriculture, North Carolina State University, 1986.

White, T. "A Study of the Influence of Plato and Aristotle on

Thomas More's *Utopia*." Unpublished doctoral dissertation, Department of Philosophy, Columbia University, 1974.

Williams, J. M. *Style: Toward Clarity and Grace*. Chicago: University of Chicago Press, 1990.

Winer, B. J. *Statistical Principles in Experimental Design*. (2nd ed.) New York: McGraw-Hill, 1971.

Zinsser, W. *On Writing Well*. (3rd ed.) New York: Perennial Library, 1988.

Ziolkowski, T. "The Ph.D. Squid." *American Scholar*, Spring 1990, pp. 177–195.

INDEX

209